A
Daughter's
Journey
Home

A
Daughter's
Journey
Home

Finding *a* Way *to* Love, Honor
and Connect *with* Your Mother

DR. LINDA MINTLE

INTEGRITY®
PUBLISHERS

Nashville

Copyright © 2004 by Linda S. Mintle, Ph.D.

Published by Integrity Publishers, a division of Integrity Media, Inc., 5250 Virginia Way, Suite 110, Brentwood, TN 37027.

HELPING PEOPLE WORLDWIDE EXPERIENCE *the* MANIFEST PRESENCE *of* GOD.

Unless otherwise indicated, Scripture quotations in this volume are taken from the Holy Bible, New International Version (NIV). Copyright © 1973, 1978, 1984, International Bible Society. Used by permission of Zondervan Bible Publishers. Other Scripture quotations are from:

The King James Version (KJV) of the Bible.

The Message (MSG), copyright 1993. Used by permission of NavPress Publishing Group.

New American Standard Bible (NASB), © 1960, 1977 by the Lockman Foundation.

The New King James Version (NKJV), copyright © 1979, 1980, 1982, 1992, Thomas Nelson, Inc., Publisher.

This book is not intended to provide therapy, counseling, clinical advice or treatment or to take the place of clinical advice and treatment from your personal physician or professional mental health provider. Readers are advised to consult their own qualified healthcare physicians regarding mental health and medical issues. Neither the publisher nor the author takes any responsibility for any possible consequences from any treatment, action or application of information in this book to the reader. Names, places, and identifying details have been changed to protect the privacy of individuals who may have similar experiences. The characters depicted here consist of composites of a number of people with similar issues, and the names and circumstances have been changed to protect their confidentiality. Any similarity between the names and stories of individuals described in this book to individuals known to readers is purely coincidental.

ISBN 1-59145-100-0 (hardcover)

Printed in the United States of America

To my mother, Esther Marquardt,
for your unwavering love and your giving heart.
Thanks for making the journey with me over the years.
I love you, Mom.
And to my daughter, Kaitlyn.
As we continue our journey together,
may you always find your way home.
Wherever you are, remember to kiss your pillow!
You are such a delight and greatly loved.

Contents

Contents

ACKNOWLEDGMENTS

DURING THE WRITING OF THIS BOOK, my mother was diagnosed with cancer for the second time in her life. During her first bout, I was ten years old and really did not comprehend the seriousness of her condition. As was typical of my mother, she fought the disease while working a full-time job and taking care of our family. Her first healing was miraculous, and she is living testimony of God's healing power. This time, the seriousness of her condition was very much realized and gave tremendous perspective to my writing.

Once again, God miraculously intervened. By the time I wrote the last lines of this book, she was again declared cancer-free. Mom, God decided to keep you with us for a while longer—and we are thankful! Over the years, your willingness to work through our rough places has helped me write the chapters of this book. Thanks for your availability, compassion, and commitment to family.

To my children and husband who found me daily glued to the computer in my home office, your patience and flexibility were greatly appreciated. Katie, my one and only daughter, I often thought

Acknowledgments

of the two of us as I wrote each chapter. I pray God will keep us both close to Him and to each other.

To my new family at Integrity Publishers, I am so grateful for our meaningful connections. Thanks for making the effort to make them, for being personable, creative, encouraging, and visionary. Joey Paul, I sit as a student at your editing feet. What a humble, gifted, and compassionate man you are. And thank you to my editor, Sue Ann Jones, who so graciously mentored me. You were a gift.

And most importantly, thanks to God, the true healer who gives insight and wisdom. It is He who melts my heart and continually challenges me to be like Him in all my relationships.

INTRODUCTION: THE RELATIONSHIP THAT AFFECTS ALL OTHERS

It BEGINS WITH A CRY. In some cases, a wail. Excruciating pain and joy all mixed together. Birth is a metaphor depicting the bond between mother and daughter. It's a relationship that can be painful— and it can also bring immense joy. And here's the really amazing thing: It affects *every* current and future relationship. That's why we have to pay attention to it and make it the best we can.

Something profound connects a daughter to the woman who responded to her cries in the night, changed her diapers, coaxed her into her first steps, acted as paramedic, went head to head with her over a thousand adolescent and teenage issues, and prayed constantly for her protection. Instinct draws the two together. As the daughter grows, her craving for autonomy increases, but the need for connection with Mom remains.

A grown-up daughter must come to terms with the fact that she is still her mother's daughter. Don't be afraid of this thought. Being your mother's daughter doesn't ultimately define you. However, it does influence who you are and your choice of life partner. In fact, feminists believe we marry our mother. Yes, I said *marry* our *mother*. Chew on *that* thought for a while!

Longing for Mom's Acceptance, No Matter What

Ideally, this primary mother-daughter bond builds intimately over the years. In reality, as adults most of us struggle to find balance in our emotional relationships with our mother.

Over the past twenty years while conducting therapy, I have listened to terrible stories of mother-daughter abuse and neglect. I've worked with daughters whose mothers locked them in closets when they were children and/or whose moms were alcoholics, mentally ill, sexually abusive, cocaine users, prostitutes. You name it, I've heard it. For many, the potential joy of the mother-daughter relationship was quickly lost in hurt and wounding, or worn away through neglect, abandonment, and other unhappy experiences. It's only through the miraculous power of God that these troubled women can even find their way to a therapy office to speak of such trauma. And yet, no matter how horrific the relationship, daughters still long for their mother's acceptance and unconditional love.

The emotional intensity between mother and daughter is an amazingly complex force. Even the best-trained therapists have no advantage when it comes to working things out with their mother. We are all clients in need of help. For me, sorting through my similarities and differences with my mother has been work—work that all daughters have to do. Like every daughter, I've had my share of disappointments and felt misunderstood. I've blamed, yelled, been angry, cried, laughed, misperceived, and experienced every emotion possible. Mom and I have definitely had our moments of contention and complaint. We are far from perfect but have found that love, faith, and a willingness to work on our relationship have brought us to a place of meaningful connection.

At midlife, I have reached a point of clearer perspective. I could not have written this book in my twenties. And being a mom has given me a much-needed appreciation for my mother's difficult task of raising me. Now, no matter what momentary entanglements Mom and I face, we work them out. In the end, we know that we are individual women who will stand before God and answer for our earthly actions. In heaven we can't make excuses by blaming others for how we behaved. ("Hello, God. Did You know my mother? Enough said; let me pass!")

BUILDING ON OUR POINTS OF CONNECTION

Here on earth, we long for that original oneness we first experienced with Mom. But inevitably our search will come up empty. We can't reenter our mother's womb and stay in that safe place. Safety and unconditional love can only be found in relationship with God—in our spiritual rebirth.

As we move forward in our mother-daughter relationship, our expectations and ideals are not always met. When those expectations come head to head with reality, we experience loss: *How could she . . . ? Why would she . . . ? I can't believe she . . . !* Our task then as daughters is to learn to accept that loss, grieve it, and move forward. We must choose to accept our mother's infallibility, feel the anger, shock, hurt, and sadness that accompany this reality—and then let go of it. Moving on may require forgiving her, adjusting our expectations, or simply coming to grips with the fact that we all make mistakes. In some cases, it may even require a new awareness that Mom has areas of woundings and hurts she's yet to face. Her own unresolved pain may still affect you. And while you can't force another person (in this case, Mom) to confront that pain and deal with it, you can control your reaction to it. Her pain doesn't have to control or define you once you learn to be uniquely you and still have a relationship with her.

We must find the points of connection that still exist with our mother and build on them. Regardless of how we perceive our mother, or what reality may be for us, we are challenged to imitate Christ in everything we do. To love as Christ loved often requires amazing grace and liberal use of forgiveness.

Through my experience and my training, my goal in these pages is to guide you into being who you were created to be while helping you enrich your connection with your mom. And I'll show you that this is possible whether you are about to graduate from school and set out on your own, or you are an adult with a family of your own, or you are a mature woman whose mother is no longer living. Even then it's still possible to examine the relationship you had with your mother, learn how it has affected who you are today, and grieve for any losses that you wish that relationship had included but didn't. Does this sound like exhausting work? It is! But the benefits are worth it.

And while my focus is on daughters who want to build a rewarding relationship with their mother, I'll also include some time- and experience-tested advice for those of you who are now the mothers of daughters at home. My goal in sharing these suggestions is not only to help you mold an intimate and rewarding relationship with your daughter but also to help you see how your own mother's interactions with you during your childhood shaped the relationship you have today.

If that relationship is less than ideal, this book will help you restore or improve it. Too many women think the solution to mother-daughter problems is relationship cutoff. They walk away or stay angrily distant from their mother. They don't talk to her or have anything to do with her. This withdrawal makes them feel in charge of their lives. However, they're confusing cutoff with being independent. You are not independent when you run away from problems. You might feel temporarily relieved, but the problems still exist. And you don't learn how to take a position and hold your ground when you run away. Relationship cutoff is often motivated by unresolved anger and bitterness, and it usually repeats itself in other relationships as well.

Other daughters stay joined at the hip, unable to resolve the emotional attachments they have to their mom. They are unable to "find their own voices," as therapists say. This is a process that's so important, it's worth a note of explanation. Finding your voice means learning who you are, identifying your feelings and thoughts, and being able to speak them in any relationship without feeling guilty or defensive. Daughters who are unable to find their voices have difficulty leaving home, both physically and emotionally. They are so tuned in to the voice of their mother, they either don't develop their own or don't pay attention to it. Knowing who you are is not dependent on another person. It is a process of discovery that is learned in relationship to God and others.

Still other daughters keep things superficial. As long as they don't talk about anything personal or emotionally laden, they can have a relationship with Mom. There are dutiful visits, but no intimacy exists.

If you are still trying to make peace with your mother, don't despair and don't give up. It has nothing to do with changing her or trying to control her. It has everything to do with you and how you respond to her. Whether your mother is still living or long gone, wonderful or abusive, you can come to terms with this powerful bond.

Introduction

Each of us must also find a way to *honor* our mother. This doesn't mean we allow abuse or don't confront difficulty. It simply means we honor the position. Scripture tells us, "'Honor your mother and father'—which is the first commandment with a promise—'that it may go well with you and that you may enjoy long life on the earth.'"[1] This isn't easy for those who have been deeply wounded. But it is necessary for emotional health.

No mother is perfect. Those of us who are now mothers are reassured by that statement. I often wonder what my daughter will say about me later in life. What moments will stand out to her as pivotal times? I hope and pray I do well. But I'm not so naive to think she won't have her own "issues" with me. Like most moms, I'm trying to do my best. Daily I pray for wisdom, discernment, and mercy and ask God to fill in the places of my failure and weakness.

Instead of spending years fused with our mother or blaming her for all our grown-up problems or becoming peeved at her imperfections or resenting her moments of hiding and making mistakes, let's build on what we have and learn to love properly. There is no perfect love apart from God. All our attempts to create perfect love through human relationship will end in futility. Does this mean we just have to accept what is and give up trying to improve our mother-daughter relationships? No, it doesn't. Otherwise I wouldn't have a book to write! But we may have to give up our never-ending efforts to change our mother into the perfect nurturers—all-knowing and all-giving—we think they need to be.

I should mention that I've read my share of psychological theories that attempt to explain why mothers and daughters have relationship cutoff. Everything from mothers' failure to breastfeed to our patriarchal society is blamed. In this book, though, I am not looking for sources to blame. And I especially don't want to blame mothers. Relationships are complex; they're lived in multiple contexts and influenced by many different factors. Most mothers I've ever known or seen in therapy don't set out to ruin their daughters' lives or purposely hope they will end up on my therapy couch. They do what they know to do. At times they fail, make bad choices, or simply repeat the patterns of their own families. Most of the time, they simply do the best they can—just as I do with my daughter.

BUILDING AND KEEPING A REWARDING RELATIONSHIP

This book is about helping daughters come to terms with their mother and develop intimate connections that can stand the test of time. No matter how awful, how good, or how in-between your mother seems to be, you can have a rewarding relationship with her while maintaining a sense of who you are. The sooner you can do this, the better off you'll be. Granted, this goal isn't necessarily an easy one to achieve. In fact, in some cases, it's extremely difficult. And it's usually a process that takes time. But it's well worth the time and effort.

So let's get started on our way to building a healthy mother-daughter relationship. Along the way, I will offer insights regarding places of "stuckness," or difficulty. The point of these insights will be to encourage you to change, to make modifications that will bring you to a place of peace when it comes to answering the question, "How do you feel about your mother?" At the end of this book, I hope you can answer that question by saying, "I am at peace with our relationship."

At the end of each chapter you'll find "Thought Points" to help you reconsider the issues raised in that chapter and apply them to your own mother-daughter relationship. They are aimed at you as an individual reader. But please be aware that the *ideal* way to use these questions is to discuss them with your mother. I know, however, that for many of you, that goal just isn't possible, either because your relationship with your mom is strained or because she is no longer living. If your mom is alive, I hope by the end of the book you will have progressed so that you *are* able to use the thought points as a means of connection with your mother. But even if this remains impossible, the questions and suggestions will help you take the necessary steps toward coming to peace with your relationship.

Women often ask me, "How will I know when I have reached a mature relationship with my mom?" My answer comes from my clinical training with the Women's Project in Family Therapy, during which family therapist and author Betty Carter helped me understand that we have made peace when we can take a personal stand on an emotionally important issue without attacking our mother or being defensive about ourselves. She also taught me that:

1. You have to come to terms with your mother and define yourself. Your mother can't do this for you.
2. Everyone feels let down by her mother, regardless of reality, because of the expectations we place on her.
3. The more you work on your relationship with your mother, the better your legacy to the next generation will be.[2]

It is my prayer that each of us will make peace with our mother, that we will choose to take this daughter's journey home and find a way to honor and cherish the woman we call Mom.

Now, Let's All Just Try to Stay Calm . . .

"How do you feel about your mother?"

"Well, since you asked *today*, I feel good about my mother. But if you had asked me last Friday, I was ready to wring her neck! And tomorrow I may want to exchange her for a different model. I love her, hate her, feel guilty, and wish I was a better daughter. How long is this session—have you got a few years?"

"My mother died when I was seven years old. She was my best friend. I often wonder what my life would be like if she had lived. I miss her terribly."

"I don't want to talk about her. She's just the woman who gave birth to me; that's how I see her. Basically she screwed up my life, and I think I probably hate her. Most times, I'm just indifferent about her. You know, sort of numb. Next question."

"I consider my mom my best friend. She's such an encourager, always there when I need her. We are so much alike, it's scary. If I can be as good a mother as she is, I'll be happy."

"Are you going to talk about how she didn't breast-feed me and weird stuff like that? Because I just want to know how to get along with my mom. Right now, that's a big problem."

"My mother? Sounds like a shrink question to me. Does it matter how I feel about her? I don't know, Dr. Linda. How do you feel about yours?"

Even though I've asked this question hundreds of times in therapy, I'm always amazed at the intense emotions it evokes. Women laugh, cry, grow silent, get deep in thought, yell, swear, smile . . . it's a simple but tough question with a complicated answer that can change from day to day.

The powerful mother-daughter bond is a hotbed for all kinds of emotions. And it doesn't much matter what age we are or if our mother is alive or deceased. When emotions run positive, the bond is like no other. But when negative emotions rear their ugly heads, poor reactions and coping can lead to depression, anxiety, anger, and a host of defensive feelings.

I LOVE MY MOM, BUT . . .

Most women tell me, "I love my mother, but . . ." And it's that "but" that trips us up. "But I don't feel close to her." "But she tries to control me." "But I can't please her." "But I have a lot of guilt." "But she won't treat me like an adult." "But I get so angry with her." The list is long.

So the question is, how do we handle these strong emotions—this emotional reactivity, as therapists call it? Can we avoid becoming emotional wrecks or stop feeling like we are ten years old again? And how can we move from a defensive posture with Mom to a more supportive one? By the time you finish this chapter, you should have answers. And by the time you finish this book, you'll have a variety of information, strategies, and methods that will help you develop a rewarding relationship with your mom.

I'm going to remind you over and over of this one helpful truth; please keep it in the back of your mind as you work through this book: You can't change your mother, but you can change your reaction to her. And when you change your reaction to Mom, it changes your interaction, which impacts your relationship. Change comes when you decide to react differently. So many daughters waste their time trying to change their mother. Let me tell you from personal experience, it's an exercise in frustration. Your mother is *not* your patient asking for help from her doctor daughter!

Our goal is to rein in our emotions and get control. We want to respond in ways that promote love and connection. Don't get caught up in what Mom is doing. Focus with me on *your* reactions. In this chapter, we'll look at ways to help you make the mother-daughter relationship more rewarding by controlling the part of your relationship you do have control over. Yes, you guessed it—your own reactions.

DEFENSE, DEFENSE

When I was a college cheerleader, we yelled the cheer, "Defense! Defense!" mostly when we were losing a game. Out of frustration, we wanted our team to defend the goal and prevent the other team from scoring. It was a strategy aimed at stopping the other team's offensive efforts. However, defense didn't put points on the board for *our* team. Consequently, a great defensive effort could still result in a lost game.

The same is true for mothers and daughters. When we put all our time and energy into defending our point of view (defending the goal), we don't encourage the building of an intimate relationship (scoring points). Defensive reactions block our communication, and as a result, intimacy is lost. When we become highly defensive or upset, we don't listen. We aren't reasonable. And all we want to do is win our point.

In this chapter, I will identify the traps that pull you into defensive communication and move you toward developing more supportive communication that is conducive to a healthy relationship.

Defensive communication usually comes about because you feel attacked, judged, guilty, fearful, or anxious. Because our mom's appraisal of us matters, we may become defensive when we think she is undercutting our sense of worth or not validating who we are—an individual who's separate and independent of her. When this happens, it can breed regret, hostility, and other strong emotions. Hostility and anger are so prevalent in mother-daughter relationships that I am devoting an entire chapter to them (see chapter 2). For now, let's understand what goes into defensive communication so we can make changes to avoid it.

EVALUATE YOUR REACTION STYLE

When you and Mom hit a point of contention in the relationship, what is your style of reacting? Do you become highly defensive? If so, what do you do when you feel attacked or judged? Your answers matter because when you respond with strong emotions, nothing gets solved. And that's not the only problem. Usually after an unpleasant, emotional confrontation with your mother, the residual emotions that you carry around can stress you out and even create physical problems. The goal here is to help you become less reactive and more responsive in your dealings with your mother. To stay calmer and more mature, you may have to practice reacting less and responding better.

So let's begin by identifying possible defensive styles. When you're dealing with your mother, do you engage in any of the responses listed below?

1. Go on the attack and then try to rationalize or justify what you said or did. In order to protect yourself from Mom, you take the offensive and attack her. That way you don't have to feel vulnerable or risk getting hurt.

2. Blame others and not take responsibility for yourself. Someone else is always at fault, and you are the perennial victim. Or even if you are at fault, you don't want to "own it." That is, you don't want to acknowledge your mistake and take responsibility for it. So you find someone or something else to blame.

3. Give in—and later regret that you did. Are you easily swayed by the person-to-person contact, then do you kick yourself later for not standing up for what you really think or believe? Are you easily persuaded because you don't really know what you think and feel?

4. Agree with Mom up-front but then go behind her back and try to get even. This is a passive-aggressive way of dealing with your mom. It's indirect and dishonest because you don't have the guts to deal directly with your disagreement; instead you find secretive ways to get back at her. You may appear to do what she wants while hiding your true actions. In other words, you give Mom the impression that you are going along with her advice, thinking, and values, but then you behave in different ways. This creates a false self—the one that Mom sees. The real self behaves very differently away from her presence.

5. Just avoid problems. There is no communication because you are avoiding the issues. Your reacting style is to pull away and with-draw. Nothing is accomplished except that you are temporarily removed from the tension. But that tension doesn't go away.

Think about what you tend to do when the heat rises in your relationship with your mother. None of the defensive styles described above will deepen intimacy or move you toward more open communication channels. If you tend to become defensive by using any of the above strategies, you need to make changes. Stop attacking, blaming, and avoiding Mom, and stop agreeing with her when you don't want to. Learn to listen and be honest and direct. As you lose your defensive posture, you'll be able to have more interactions that are less volatile. Here are some tips to help you do that.

Identify the Triggers

Most of us have emotional triggers that send us into orbit with Mom. Triggers are those things that set off, or cue, an emotional reaction in you. They can be specific events, conversations, or people; they can be your thoughts or Mom's behavior. Here's an easy example. Let's say every time you try a new fashion idea, Mom makes a negative comment, a put-down. So you learn that expressing yourself through fashion is bound to bring criticism and thus is a trigger.

Here's another example. Your mother calls to complain that "nobody" cares about her because *you* don't call her every day. She fails to mention that you have three sisters who could pay attention to her needs as well. Whenever she makes these self-pitying comments, you feel really guilty and apologize out of a sense of obligation. Later, you get upset with yourself for playing this emotional game. (This is number three on the previous list of defensive strategies.) The truth is, you haven't been ignoring your mom, and your sisters haven't done their part. But her phone calls trigger an overwhelming sense of dread and guilt in you.

Think about this example. You were deeply hurt over your mom's comments about working outside the home. You are a single mom and must work to support your children, but your mother keeps bringing up her wish that you would marry and be able to stay home. Because you are stressed and worry about being a single parent, you blow up at her. The trigger is your thought, *She thinks I'm a bad mother for having to go to work. I don't need to hear this. I already feel bad enough.*

Your thoughts may not be based in reality, but you attribute blame to her anyway.

While these are examples of specific triggers that might be at work, there are also common triggers that send many of us into a defensive state. Usually they include three general areas:

1. Triggers related to our feelings.

2. Triggers related to *not* dealing with our own "stuff" (that is, the issues in our lives that incite strong emotions within us).

3. Triggers related to Mom's not dealing with her own stuff. (Be careful here. Most daughters would like to believe this is the main problem when it may not be.)

Check this list. Think about the times and situations when intense negative feelings are triggered in you. What triggers those reactions? Ask yourself if it usually involves one or more of these issues:

Feelings

The feeling may or may not be based in reality, but this is how you feel:

- unsupported
- unaccepted or unapproved
- misunderstood
- frustrated
- insecure
- obligated

Your Stuff

Your problems that might trigger strong emotions in your mom could include:

- refusing to see your part in the problem (a situation that leads to unfair blame, denial, rationalizing, and anger)
- suggesting motives that don't exist
- projecting (putting) your feelings onto Mom (confusing your stuff with hers)
- failing to understand and listen
- not seeing the big picture (see chapter 5)

Mom's Stuff

Your mom's behaviors that could trigger strong emotions in you might include:

- critical, sarcastic put-downs
- invalidating your feelings, that is, minimizing them to the point that you believe you "shouldn't" feel a certain way
- using unfair blame or guilt
- excessive control
- avoidance of problems
- playing the martyr
- frail and unable to cope

How to Respond to Triggers

Now, you can't control your mother's thoughts or behaviors. And you can't force her to deal with her "stuff." Her reactions are just that—

her reactions. So stop trying to change her, unless she's *asking* to change and wants your feedback. Most likely, *you* will be the one changing in order to create a more rewarding relationship. Remember, you can't control her reaction, but you can control *your* response to her reaction. So let's focus on how to respond to these emotional triggers.

Practice Taking Fire

Once you have identified the specific triggers that set off an intense emotional reaction in you, practice a new way to respond to those triggers. In therapy, I often have my clients act out or role-play a typical triggered event. Then we rehearse a new way to handle that specific issue.

For example, Mary loses it every time her mom brings up her divorce. Mary knows her mom won't stop talking about the divorce, and now she realizes it is a trigger for her to go on the defensive. So, in therapy, Mary thinks through a better way to react to Mom's comments. She decides to say, "Mom, I'm disappointed by the divorce too. When you bring it up, it makes me feel even worse. There is nothing I can do about it now but grieve it as a loss. He's left me for another woman. I could really use your support to get through this. One way you could support me is to not keep reminding me how much I have failed. Instead help me face the future."

Mary then coaches me to be her mom, sharing what Mom usually says and how she acts. I then play her mother, and she practices her new strategy. She is less defensive because she states how she feels and asks for constructive help. Her mom can choose to ignore her request and continue her divorce-track comments, so I take this position and allow Mary to practice handling this possibility. We rehearse as many scenarios as Mary can think up. The rehearsal helps Mary think through her responses when she's not so defensive so that she can have a more controlled reaction when her mom inevitably brings up the topic.

Rehearsing your responses ahead of time prepares you for the next time the trigger occurs. You may still lose it and go on the defensive from time to time, but with practice, you can eventually learn to respond differently.

Develop Assertiveness and Self-Definition

You'll read this lesson repeatedly throughout this book: The more you understand who you are apart from your mom, the better you can be true to yourself when you are with her. So an important step to controlling your emotions when you respond to her is to work on developing yourself as a unique person apart from your mom. This means defining your beliefs and letting your own personality prevail. Therapists call this process defining your "I" and finding your voice. (We'll discuss these processes in more detail in later chapters.) Work on your reactions to emotionally charged issues. Remember, the goal is to be less defensive and more honest in your relationship. In order to be honest, you have to know what you think and feel.

In the earlier example concerning fashion as a trigger for criticism, there are several ways to respond that won't lead you down an angry and defensive path. First, since you have identified the emotional trigger, practice how you will respond to it. Be prepared to be assertive. It helps to keep your response *descriptive* versus *judging*. Describe your own feelings rather than attacking your mom for being critical. For example, you might say something like, "Mom, I like to have fun with fashion. It hurts when you criticize me about it. If you don't like my style, I would prefer you keep your comments to yourself since it creates bad feelings." In this case, you are asserting who you are (you're using your voice), but not in a defensive way. Your reaction isn't an angry, impulsive backlash but rather a true *description* of how you feel and a request for her to change. Mom's response is up to her, but at least you've given her a strategy that would help the relationship.

You can take your position without having to prove anything because you are only describing what happens to you. This requires you to spend some time gathering knowledge about yourself (the self-definition work) and to be somewhat introspective about your behavior and thoughts. When you are comfortable with your choices, you may feel more secure and have greater willingness to be open to feedback; you may be willing to think about Mom's comments and decide if there is any merit in them—you can listen without becoming highly defensive. This practice of defining yourself and then "using your voice" can help control your negative reactions to your mom.

The groundwork for some daughters is to take time and really think about what they do think and feel. That was the case for Rhonda. We had numerous sessions in which all she would do was go on the attack about her mother. When I pushed her to stop complaining and tell me what she wanted to change and how that would look, she didn't know what to say. She had spent so much of her life being upset and lambasting her Mom that she didn't have a clue what she actually wanted the relationship to be like.

Hey, That's Not What the Bible Says!

When my kids were little, one of my favorite books to read to them was one entitled *Hey, That's Not What the Bible Says!* by Bill Ross. The author takes a Bible story and then gives it a wrong ending. You read the incorrect ending and turn the page, and a bunch of kids are screaming, "Hey, that's not what the Bible says!" Then the author corrects the story's ending.

The reason I like this book so much is that it reminds me of life. We tend to make up our own endings to relationship problems. In our version, people are apologizing for wrong actions, being fair, addressing issues when they arise, and basically living in the epitome of mental health and applying their Christian faith flawlessly. Well, as we all know, life isn't like that. Instead, we have to cope with all the "incorrect endings." When we face denial, injustice, poor treatment, lack of validation, etc., our work is to respond as Christ would respond. When we don't, we need to imagine God saying, "Hey, that's not what the Bible says!"

Biblical relationship guidelines are healthy and foster communication. But they aren't usually our first instinctual response. However, the benefits of responding to others in a Christlike way are amazing. Not only will your relationships improve, but so will your mental health. We don't call Jesus the Great Physician for nothing!

When you are negatively triggered by something in the relationship with your mom, try not to react without thinking. Don't act impulsively or give vent to your frustrations. Unconsciously, we probably believe that Mom will take whatever we sling at her. Because of this trust, too often we tend to let loose rather than use self-control.

It's easy to take offense. Harder not to. Easy to react. Harder to respond in a godly, loving way. I speak from experience.

Personally, I've made it my goal to assess whether my actions and reactions line up with God's Word. Since the Bible directs us to respond in ways that often are counter to our human nature, we have to constantly check our reactions against the Word, admit when we've failed, and try again. It isn't easy. But hey, I figure that's the work of walking out my faith. No one said it would be easy!

So how do you stop being so defensive with Mom? Start reading the Bible and absorb what is said about being loving, kind, gentle, patient, longsuffering, self-controlled, faithful, and peaceful. This is the "fruit," or outcome, of what should be evidenced when we are one of His. It only comes when we have intimacy with God and put the Word in our hearts.[1]

And then there is the wisdom of Scripture—the grandest Ann Landers of all time. If you just consider the wisdom offered in Proverbs alone (not to mention the rest of the Bible), it will keep you on your toes. Here is a taste of that wisdom from Proverbs:

1. **Incline your ear to wisdom, and apply your heart to understanding (2:2, NKJV).** When we try to understand the situation, the bigger picture, the heat of the moment, or whatever the circumstances of an emotional interaction, it helps us stay calmer. Understanding goes a long way in any relationship, because when we have understanding, we tend to be more tolerant and empathetic.

2. **Don't talk too much, for it fosters sin. Be sensible and turn off the flow! (10:19, NLT).** OK, I admit this is a tough one for me, but one I keep working on. The point is, hold your tongue so you don't say things in haste that you may later regret.

3. **A kindhearted woman gains respect, but ruthless men gain only wealth (11:16).** Do you think of yourself as kindhearted? Ready to give the benefit of the doubt and look for positives in your mom? If not, you may gain other things such as wealth or material possessions but at a high cost. Is losing respect worth being ruthless? Or would you rather be kindhearted and gain her respect?

4. **Reckless words pierce like a sword, but the tongue of the wise brings healing (12:18).** Back to our tongues again! The Bible has lots to say about this small part of our body that can do so much damage. The lesson here is, don't be reckless in what you say; don't lash out, hurt, wound, or say mean things because *you* feel hurt or wounded. Choose your words carefully so they can be part of healing and not hurting.

5. Pride only breeds quarrels, but wisdom is found in those who take advice (13:10). There are times our mother is right and we become defensive because we don't want to hear it. The root of this is usually pride, and pride breeds quarrels.

6. He who answers before listening—that is his folly and his shame (18:13). One of the problems of defensiveness is that you don't hear what is being said. If all you are doing is planning what you will say and how you will defend yourself, you really can't hear what your mom is trying to say. Listen first, *then* think about what you want to say.

The Bible is full of instructions and wisdom concerning our responses to relationship difficulties. The point is to use the Bible as a guide for *your responses* to Mom rather than as a club to judge and criticize her. When you line up your thoughts and actions with biblical teachings, you won't be operating out of defensiveness but out of a sense of God-given love and self-control.

Learn to Problem-Solve

When you find yourself in a heated moment with your mom, try problem-solving. Here are the basic steps to take when a problem comes your way.

1. Define the problem. Define a clear and specific behavior, then in a nonaccusatory way, describe what is happening. By clearly targeting the problem, you both will know you aren't working with some nebulous thing. For example, instead of saying, "Mom, you are such an avoider," be concrete. Say, "Mom, when I try to talk about your health, you change the subject." First define the problem; focus on the behavior so you'll know what needs to change.

For years I taught a parenting course. In that course, I taught parents how to define behavior problems with their children. To help them learn this skill I followed this procedure: I asked each parent to give me his or her recipe for meatloaf. Some made it with breadcrumbs and eggs; others used barbecue sauce. All kinds of ingredients showed up in the recipes; they differed from parent to parent. So when I would talk about *meatloaf*, all the parents had their own ideas about what that meant, depending on their personal recipe. When we communicate with our mother about a problem in our relationship, we need to avoid the meatloaf approach. Instead, we need to define the ingredients so Mom knows exactly what we are talking about.

2. How often or how long is it happening? Measure the number of times the problem occurs or the length of time it goes on. This way you will have an accurate count or duration of the problem. This is important because you need to be able to measure change as it happens. Too many of us don't recognize small changes in the right direction when they occur. For example, the daughter in the previous example might say, "The last three times I tried to bring up the subject of your health, you changed the subject."

3. Do *something*. When it's time to intervene, instead of reacting the way you always do, or in a way that doesn't promote change, try a new strategy. For example, instead of getting upset and walking away, try being firm and saying, "Mom, I really want to talk about your health. Can we do that now?" Stop doing whatever wasn't working and try a new tactic. You can experiment until you find something that works. In this example, the daughter didn't allow her mom's avoidance to upset her to the point of walking away and dropping the subject. She took a deep breath, stayed involved in the situation, and gently pushed for a response. And as suggested earlier, it helps to rehearse your new response ahead of time.

4. Evaluate how well things are going. After you have a clear idea of the problem, measure how much of a problem it is, and then act differently, you can evaluate whether the situation is improving. If your mom willingly talks about her health one time in the next two times you bring it up, you've made progress. Remember, change is usually a step-by-step process that takes time.

5. If what you are doing doesn't work, try another tactic. The secret here is not to panic or give up. You tried something, and it didn't work. Try something else. Talk to other people, a counselor or family members, and get input if you need it. Be careful not to bring others into the fray; just get some new ideas about what might work. Just because *you* don't see a solution, doesn't mean there isn't one. There is always a way. Remember, this is also a promise from God. He makes a way where there is no way, so don't panic or give up.

Practice problem-solving. It will boost your confidence and reduce your feelings of defensiveness. Next time you feel yourself becoming defensive, tell yourself, *I can deal with this. It's just a matter of finding the right solution. God, help me to find a better way.*

Lighten Up

When you are triggered by an emotional issue with your mom, one of your best responses is to use humor. When used appropriately, humor can diffuse tension and lighten the moment. It allows both parties to laugh and gain a fresh perspective for the moment. Of course, you don't want to use humor to laugh off problems or avoid dealing with an issue.

Here's an example of how I used humor one summer when my parents came for a visit and tension was rising between my mom and me over a particular issue. One of my triggers had to do with my mom telling me when she thought I needed to go to bed. At about 10:00 p.m., my mom would say, "Linda, don't you think it's about time you go to bed?"

At this point in my life, I had been married a number of years, had no children, and worked a full-time therapy job. Because of the distance, I only saw my parents a few times a year. I used to wonder if Mom had forgotten that I was a grownup.

In the past, when my mom would do this, I would get angry. This time, I decided to use humor instead. It really was pretty funny that my mom thought she had to tell her thirty-year-old daughter when to go to bed!

Of course, my take on the matter was that my mom was trying to control me and tell me what I needed to do. I was a grown woman and didn't need her to do this. Her take was that it's tough to ever stop being a mother. She was just concerned that I get the rest I needed and that I didn't feel obliged to stay up late with her and Dad. But because none of this was ever verbalized, we reacted to our own separate thoughts.

So, instead of my usual, "Oh, Mother!" and stomping off while mumbling under my breath, I decided to take the humorous approach. One night at ten o'clock when my mother reminded me of bedtime, instead of getting mad, I humorously said, "Oh, Mom, thanks for telling me. What would I have done if you hadn't been here? Maybe I would never go to bed. I'd be up all night. Good thing I have you here to help me." And I started to laugh. So did she. We both saw how crazy we were acting—me to get so worked up over something so inane that could easily have been handled had I simply asked why she did this. She was feeling the need to take care of me. She saw my pressured life and wanted to help.

As we laughed, she said, "I guess you never stop being a mother and caring for your kids. It's hard to make the transition." And I was reminded how much she really did care about me and how often she had helped me as a child. I realized she was motivated by love and not control.

17

Taking Time-Outs

One of the most effective parenting strategies for kids who react defensively to a situation is giving them a time-out. The purpose of a time-out is to stop the observed inappropriate behavior and give the child time to cool down and think about what he or she did.

Adults need to employ this strategy as well. Use it with your mom when an interaction heats up and you feel you're losing it. Simply say, "I'm getting too worked up to be sane. I need a few minutes of time-out." Then walk away and cool down. Take a few deep breaths, pray, count to ten, and *think*. Define the problem and consider what you are reacting to. You've been triggered—now how do you want to respond?

Wait until you have calmed down, then go back to the problem and deal with it. Don't wait a week or months. Get back to it as soon as you feel able to be calmer in the relationship. Most of the time, a twenty-minute cooling-off period will be enough.

Drop the Rope

As we grow in maturity with our mom, we eventually learn to accept her faults versus resent them. It seems we have fewer tensions because we begin to see our mom as an individual woman and not just as a parent.

The more you can tell your mom you care about her, the better. Show gratitude for what she has done and the sacrifices she has made. This goes a long way to cutting through defenses. No one likes to be criticized all the time, even if it is justified. Praise and acts of affection help to create an atmosphere in which problems can be raised and addressed.

If being around your mom for any period of time is difficult, then plan your visits to be short and structured. This is often the advice I give daughters who come from abusive or addicted homes who want to maintain a tie with their mom but don't want to position themselves to be hurt again. In those cases, it may even be appropriate to stay in a hotel so you have a place to which you can retreat and compose yourself. Explain this to your mom by saying, "I want to see you, but I feel it's best if I have my own space while I'm here." Then visit Mom on your terms, leaving if you find her in a physically altered state (by drugs or alcohol, for instance) or abusive. Tell her ahead of time (when she is thinking clearly) that if she is altered by her addiction or becomes abusive, you will need to leave.

In less-dangerous situations, there are mother-daughter issues that sometimes *can't* be resolved. In those cases, therapist Betty Carter tells us to metaphorically let go of the rope. In other words, you may want to drop the issue to make peace. When you encounter extreme resistance and your mom is unwilling to relent, the best strategy may be to agree to disagree and build the relationship around other relationship points.

For example, one adult daughter I worked with couldn't stand the second husband her mom married. She felt as though this man was a gold digger and using her mom for her money. She tried to talk to her mom about him, but her mom refused to even consider her daughter's ideas. Mom made it clear that she was married to this man, and the marriage was not negotiable. If she had made a mistake, she'd live with it, and she didn't want her daughter intruding. She appreciated her daughter's concern but didn't want her help in this area.

Mother and daughter agreed to avoid the topic of the new second husband. And while this put some strain in the relationship, the daughter concentrated on staying connected to Mom despite Mom's new status. She agreed to drop the rope.

The second-husband issue could have been an ongoing battle, but the daughter decided to make peace with Mom. Her mom knew where her daughter stood concerning the second husband, and the daughter knew Mom was a grownup and had to make her own love life decisions. In this case, the daughter agreed to drop the rope regarding a specific issue that could potentially block her mother-daughter relationship. She didn't *avoid* the problem—she told her mother how she felt—but she did recognize that this was an issue from which her mother would not budge. Her mother had made that clear: she was unwilling to entertain her daughter's views on this topic.

Sort through the Laundry of Guilt

Could there ever be a book about mothers and daughters that doesn't talk about guilt when it comes to defensive reactions? If you are a daughter, you have guilt over something! Guilt is like laundry. It just seems to pile up. To keep it from taking over the laundry room—or your relationship with your mom—you have to sort through it.

On the one hand, guilt is a good thing. It prevents us from continuing to misbehave or act out. We train our children to feel guilty when they've been disobedient. Ideally, guilt leads to confession of wrongdoing and repentance. True guilt should lead to change.

If you feel guilty because you've done something to hurt your mom, good. Go make it right. Don't just stare at your navel and feel badly. Take action.

Jennifer had to do this. She felt extremely guilty for lying to her mom about a recent financial situation. A multitude of bad choices had left Jennifer in overwhelming debt. She was advised by an attorney to declare bankruptcy and was embarrassed to tell her mother. The guilt was getting to her. Every time she spoke to her mom, she felt she had to cover her lie. Her dishonesty was changing their relationship in a negative way. The solution was easy, though humbling. Jennifer had to go to her mom and tell her the truth. Then she asked for forgiveness. When she did, her mom was disappointed and felt betrayed by Jennifer's dishonesty. Mom forgave Jennifer, but it took time to trust Jennifer again. However, Jennifer no longer carried around the heavy load of guilt.

On the other hand, guilt can be misplaced and unhealthy when we hang on to it and it isn't due to sin or misbehaving but rather, is due to a failure to accept our limitations. Daughters often feel guilty over not being perfect daughters.

You may be holding on to unrealistic expectations, a topic we'll discuss in chapter 5. You can't be and do everything perfect as a daughter. You will and probably have made mistakes. That's OK, as long as you admit those mistakes, ask for forgiveness, and move on. Once you sort through the laundry, put it in the machine and let it get clean. You do this by confessing, repenting, and changing.

Jesus paid the price to cleanse you. When you ask Him to take away your sin, He does it—and doesn't remember it anymore. It's gone, clean, forgiven, over, done, in the past, and never to be remembered.

You may also need to work on changing your expectations. For example, can you really call your mom every single day? Is that healthy? Or do you need some separation? Can you always be there for her every need? Should you be? Perhaps your father, brother, or sister should pitch in to help. Will you always act in ways that she approves? Probably not, because you are two different people. Do you have guilt over her not accepting every part of you?

These questions are important to ask because so much guilt comes from not living up to a certain standard either determined by you or your mom. In reality, we have only One to please: God. If you live your life according to His directives, He will honor you and be pleased. If it's at all possible, find out your mother's expectations of you by asking her what they are. Then try to negotiate if you feel they are unrealistic. Talk about what you realistically can do in the relationship.

I remember treating a young woman whose mother was upset with her because she wasn't sexually active. It sounds bizarre, but the mother was divorced and sleeping around. Mom's guilt was lessened by trying to bring the daughter into her lifestyle. Fortunately, the daughter saw this as crazy and refused to join her mother. Still, she struggled with guilt when her mom called her a prude. But the guilt was only momentary as she grounded herself in Scripture and confirmed that she was acting according to her beliefs. It's ironic but true: taking a stance against your mom, even when your mom acts crazy, can still induce guilt.

If your mom tries to throw your past in your face, simply tell her to stop. You've dealt with the past, and she needs to stop bringing up what was already forgiven and or reconciled. If you keep bringing up the past, you aren't playing fair either. The past, once resolved, needs to stay in the past.

While intellectually we can say, "Yes, God forgives me," living that out can be hard to do. Inappropriate guilt keeps us stuck, unable to move forward in the things God has for today and the future. God wants you free from guilt and shame—not so you can sin and exercise a form of cheap grace but so the true power of the cross can be revealed in your life. Embrace guilt when it leads to true repentance. Say good-bye to it when it leads to emotional captivity.

How do you stop feeling guilty? By releasing it to God. There is no magic formula here. Letting go of guilt happens when you recognize that the cross was sufficient for all your sins and you confess them. Hanging on to guilt is like saying Christ's sacrifice wasn't enough for you. Don't be misled. He died for all your sins. Confession, as the saying goes, is good for the soul because it gives you a fresh start. It is His amazing love that keeps us from condemnation.

The more you can practice moving out of defensive communication with your mom, the more your relationship will improve. And even if she never changes, you will have the satisfaction and practice of using more supportive communication. This is beneficial to all your relationships. You will also be rewarded for your attempts to be like Christ in all you do. That road is never easy, but it is the right way to proceed. Ask God to empower you to be more like Him in all you do.

Thought Points

1. What style do you tend to embrace when you become defensive with your mother?

2. What triggers send you into a defensive posture?

3. What do you want and expect from your mother-daughter relationship?

4. Study James 3 and consider how you can live out the principles shared there in your relationship with your mother.

5. Choose an issue that has caused conflict with your mother and try to problem-solve it.

6. Is there an issue in which you need to "drop the rope"?

7. Evaluate your relationship with your mother. Do you feel guilty about anything? If so, consider whether that guilt is healthy or unhealthy. If it's unhealthy, take steps to release it.

2

ANGER AT OUR IMPOSSIBLE MOTHERS

Jᴇɴɴʏ ᴡᴀs ᴄʀʏɪɴɢ as her two-year-old stood in the kitchen and screamed at the top of her lungs, "I hate you!" Horrified by those three angry words, Jenny believed something was terribly wrong. What had happened to her sweet little darling who couldn't give Mommy enough kisses in a day? Who was this foreigner stomping her feet and looking like the antichrist?

I looked at Jenny and smiled. "Your daughter is two. Telling her she can't watch her video is not what she wanted to hear. Two-year-olds don't like the word *no* and often lash out with their two-year-old mind and vocabulary. I know it feels bad, but she doesn't really hate you, Jenny. Trust me, a half-hour from now, you'll be the 'best mommy in the whole world.'"

ANGER's POWER TO MOTIVATE

Whether you are two or fifty-two, it doesn't matter. Mother-daughter anger is real. We yell it, scream it, keep it hidden, let it simmer, deny it, minimize it, hate it, swallow it, don't want it, and try to control it. Some days are better than others, but all mother-daughter pairs experience anger. Whether it's an angry moment, a chronic problem, an angry incident, or an angry person, anger is powerful and can either motivate you to change or become a stumbling block to your emotional health.

Because of the intensity of the mother-daughter bond, and because mothers are usually safe targets for our emotional expression (that is, daughters instinctively believe their mother will continue to love them even when the daughters unleash their anger on Mom), angry feelings come easily. We all feel angry at times with our impossible mother! It's normal. It's part of our human nature—a part that needs to be controlled, managed, and resolved. Otherwise anger can take on a life of its own, creating all sorts of problems.

Patricia's comments about her mom ring true for many: "My mom is impossible! I find myself reacting to her with anger far more often than I would like. Little things set me off, and I just fly off the handle. It's like she has this power over me. When I'm around her, I become this other person. At work, I'm calm and rational, but when I'm with my mother, I feel like her little girl again. It sounds crazy. When she does something that one of my friends does, I explode at her. I wouldn't explode at my friend. I just want to be the grown-up person I am and stop feeling so angry around her."

Anger, if allowed to simmer, will turn to resentment and bitterness. And serious physical and emotional consequences can result from anger gone unchecked: hypertension, chronic headaches, gastrointestinal distress, cardiac problems, strained relationships, and family conflict, just to name a few. So the best thing you can do is release anger when it happens.

Easier said than done, right? So how *do* we deal with anger toward our mom?

Unfinished Business

Most of us desire to be grown up and handle our anger in a mature way. Sometimes we have to look to the past before we can manage anger in the present because anger can be related to unfinished business from childhood. If you and your mother haven't resolved conflicts from the past, the anger attached to those hurts and wounds can stay with you for a lifetime. It's like carrying around baggage with no place to check it.

This was the case with Rosa, a depressed and lonely woman who felt her life was going nowhere. Single and divorced, she desperately wanted to be married. But when relationships became intimate, her anger drove men away.

In therapy she began to talk about the anger she felt. The normal irritations of dating seemed to loom larger than they should. Rosa demanded focused attention from men and wanted them to sacrifice their time to be with her. She knew this often caused men to leave her because they felt she wanted more than they could give. It seemed that no amount of attention satisfied her. Her angry demands were hard for suitors to swallow.

As she began talking about her mother (a subject she felt was unrelated), the root of her anger was clear. Growing up, she had never felt special, and she believed her mom cared more about her sister than about Rosa. For years, she harbored angry feelings toward her mom over this. Now that her sister was married and had a family of her own, Mom seemed to be even more enamored with her.

Because Rosa was single, she assumed almost total care for her mom as her mother aged and her health declined. As her mother demanded more of Rosa's time, Rosa came to resent her role of caretaker. But guilt kept her from being able to establish appropriate boundaries and have a life of her own. Now meeting men was difficult because so much of her time was spent with Mom. And when she did date a man, she took on the role of her mother, expecting him to take care of her. When he failed to make her feel special and important, she became angry, and then usually he disappeared from her life. The rejection further increased her lack of feeling special.

Although Rosa's anger was really with her mother, she couldn't bring herself to admit it. Her father had died early in her life. Rosa's childhood longing to feel special and cared about left her imagining that her father would have bestowed that kind of attention on her. She looked to her mother to fill this void, but Mom was too busy trying to survive financially.

Now that Rosa found herself divorced, single, and depressed, she knew her mom was disappointed in the turn her life had taken. Her mother's advice was to find a man. But in the meantime, Rosa's mom took up most of Rosa's time. Still wanting to be special in Mom's eyes, Rosa accepted the caretaker role and told her sister not to help. Meanwhile, resentment continued to grow inside her.

For all her effort, Mom saw Rosa as dutiful, not special. Rosa became angry but kept the anger hidden, always trying to get her mother to say something nice about her because of the daily sacrifices she made to support her. When her mother didn't treat her as special, Rosa looked to men to fill this void.

The work for Rosa was to acknowledge her anger at her mom and grieve the loss of being the "special daughter." As we talked about Rosa's mom, it became clear how hurt Rosa was under all her anger. The fact was, Mom was not going to think of Rosa as special. Rosa could hang on to her anger and allow it to keep influencing her male relationships and her mood, or she could decide to release it, set realistic boundaries, and enlist her sister's help. Fortunately, Rosa decided it was time to put her anger to rest.

When a mother doesn't do what you think she should do, anger can result. It is your decision as to what you will do with that anger. You can wait and hope she will change. But in most cases, this isn't likely. Or you can choose to release your anger and move forward with your life. This chapter will help you do just that.

UNRESOLVED ANGER BECAUSE OF DEATH

Some of you who are reading this have another kind of unresolved anger. Your mother is deceased, yet ghosts from the past seem to haunt you: you are eaten up by leftover anger. Perhaps your mother's death made you realize how angry you were with her when she was alive. It's not uncommon for angry recollections to surface after a parent's death.

Whatever led to your unresolved anger, when you continue to carry it with you, it's like a dark cloud hovering constantly overhead. The only way to make peace with it is to release it. Even though your mother is gone, there are ways to discharge that anger and not allow it to negatively affect you anymore.

One of those ways is to do an exercise that therapists often use. It involves writing a letter to your mom or talking to an empty chair or a picture of her. Maybe this sounds a little crazy, but it really isn't. Writing a letter or talking to a picture helps you address in death what you didn't address in life. What is it you still need to say, admit, or ask forgiveness over? Has she hurt you in unspeakable ways? If so, you'll need to move through the forgiveness process outlined in chapter 9.

In your letter, try to write down your feelings and describe any unresolved issues from when she was alive. Read that letter and allow whatever emotion you feel to surface. If anger is a part of that, let it out. Most times, the anger will lead to hurt and tears. It's appropriate—and healthy—to grieve. Finally, pray and choose to let go of the offenses and hurts.

Are you angry that your mother died? That's OK too. Perhaps you miss her greatly and wish you could call her and talk to her. Maybe you are mad at God for taking her "too soon." Whatever the case, you can express your anger in writing or in talking to her picture or to that empty chair, imagining she is sitting in it. A flood of emotion may well up. Let it come. If this all feels too intense for you to handle alone, seek out a therapist who can help you.

Whatever keeps your anger alive can be put to death if you are willing to release it. Grace and forgiveness are key. The bottom line is, unresolved anger issues, whether involving a living or deceased mother, need to be addressed and released.

Is Anger Biblical?

Some women of faith argue that anger is not biblical. That's a ridiculous statement. God's Word tells us He gets angry, and we are made in His likeness. In fact, in the Old and New Testaments there are seventy-five references to God's anger! Most of these references are directed toward those involved in idol worship and disobedience. God does get angry, but in terms of dealing with us, He is slow to anger, gracious and merciful. This is a model we are to imitate.

Think about all the human examples of anger found in the Bible, for example, the anger of the people of Nazareth toward Jesus (see Luke 4:28), Cain's anger toward his brother Abel (see Genesis 4:5–8), Saul's anger toward his son Jonathan (see 1 Samuel 20:30–34), and Paul's anger toward Ananias (see Acts 23:3). Biblical examples speak to our human makeup—we get angry—and it provides examples and guidelines as to how to handle this emotion.

The issue is not whether you *have* anger (you are in denial if you think you never do), but what you do with anger when you have it. In relationships, you don't want to unthinkingly vent your full-blown anger on someone you love (or on anyone, for that matter), but you also don't want to hang on to anger and allow it to grow into bitterness.

Whatever the cause of your anger, it's time to deal with it and live a more peaceful life. Begin by acknowledging that your anger exists. So many adult daughters I see won't admit they feel anger toward their mom. Oh, they become frustrated, upset, and mildly irritated but not angry. They believe feeling anger is somehow wrong or evil! It's neither. It's just an emotion; by itself it's not bad or good. But as mentioned before, what you do with that emotion *can* be wrong and hurtful.

Ask yourself the questions below. Use them to think more about the role anger plays in your relationship with your mother and decide if this is an area you need to work on. This list isn't exhaustive, but it should stimulate your thoughts and help you assess the role anger plays in your relationship.

1. Do I become easily angered with my mom?
   Yes   No

2. Does anger seem to be the dominant emotion in our relationship?
   Yes   No

3. Do I feel like anger is controlling me?
   Yes   No

4. Do I lash out physically toward my mom?
   Yes   No

5. Does she lash out physically toward me?
   Yes   No

6. Do we have a history of physical abuse with each other?
   Yes   No

7. Do I feel I have to defend myself most of the time?
   Yes   No

8. Is she verbally abusive with me?
   Yes   No

9. Am I verbally abusive to her?
   Yes   No

10. Do we have a history of verbal abuse?
    Yes   No

11. Do I have difficulty listening to her because I am so angry?
    Yes   No

12. Do I usually find fault with her?
    Yes   No

13. Do I have temper problems?
    Yes   No

14. Do I usually have to apologize for becoming angry?
    Yes   No

15. Do I feel disgust or contempt for her?
    Yes   No

16. Do I blame her for most of my problems?
    Yes   No

17. Am I argumentative and irritable with her?
    Yes   No

18. Does either of us feel resentful, envious, or jealous of the other?
    Yes   No

19. Am I uncooperative?
    Yes   No

20. Do I have trouble feeling empathy for my mom?
    Yes   No

21. Do I harbor unforgiveness toward her, carry a grudge, or feel bitter?
    Yes   No

22. Do I think I have an anger problem?
    Yes   No

23. Do I think Mom has an anger problem?
    Yes   No

24. Do other people think either of us has anger problems?
    Yes   No

25. Do I feel powerful when I'm angry ?
    Yes   No

26. Do I swallow my anger and keep it hidden?
    Yes   No

If you answered yes to any of these questions, you may need to work on your anger issues or learn to respond better to those of your mom. Remember, change is possible. And even though you can't change her, you can change your reaction to her.

WHAT SETS YOU OFF?

Have you ever wondered, *Why do I get so angry at my mom? I don't want to react so intensely, but I just do.* Daughters feel angry with their mom for all kinds of reasons. Among the most common triggers are our perceptions and beliefs that follow these lines of thought:

I'm angry at my mom because . . .

1. She didn't meet my needs.
2. She wanted more than I could give.
3. She reacts negatively to my choices.
4. She offers suggestions, advice, or opinions when I don't want them.
5. She's aging.
6. She intrudes upon my space and time.
7. She tries to control me.
8. She criticizes what I do.
9. She doesn't accept me for who I am.
10. She betrayed my trust or violated boundaries.

All or some of these statements may be true. Knowing what makes you feel angry can help. Considering these questions may cause you to think about your expectations of your mom. We'll discuss expectations in chapter 5 in more detail, but for now it's sufficient to remember that expectations can be unrealistic. You may be waiting for your mom to turn into someone she'll never be. It's better to accept who she is and then adjust your reactions to her. It's the only part of your relationship you can really control anyway.

For example, if she is critical of you, you know that her criticism will be an anger trigger for you. So decide ahead of time how you are going to handle her criticism. Change your response. Stop doing the same thing that leads you to an explosion. The following letter may help you see how this works.

Dear Dr. Linda:

I am a Christian woman who comes from a seriously dysfunctional family. My mother was terribly abusive to only me, and my father was absent. They divorced when I was fifteen. I have done A LOT of work on forgiving her for the past and have healed myself from that for the most part. However, because of my mother's guilt, or who knows what else, we cannot talk or be together without it becoming ugly. The only reason I have anything to do with her is to bring my daughter to holidays. I do this out of guilt and responsibility. I haven't wanted to have anything to do with my mother or my family for a long time. I have forgiven them, prayed for them, but have no desire to get together with them for any reason, especially to see my mother. Now that my daughter is grown up, she doesn't want to visit them either, especially since she would have to go by herself. I have tried so many times and in so many ways to have relationships with my family, but it never works, and I am tired of beating my head against a brick wall. I have prayed about it, for now I am peaceful not having any contact.

The primary dysfunction of the family is they never discuss any problems or issues to clear the air. They expect everyone to show up on holidays and be totally superficial like nothing is wrong. I feel like the only conscious person who wants to clear things up but I can't do it myself. In good conscience, I cannot pretend everything is OK and spend my holidays with those who barely tolerate me and don't celebrate me. As a Christian, I am conflicted about this but feel I can't expose myself to this abusive and toxic situation. What do you think?

Tammy

My response to Tammy suggests that she take some new steps in her mother-daughter relationship:

Dear Tammy,

You aren't in this boat alone. There are many women in similar situations wondering what to do. They want a relationship with their mom but don't want to be abused again and repeat the same old dysfunctional patterns of the past. You have not been—and probably never will be—able to change your family. I know you know this, but sometimes it takes our hearts longer than our heads to accept the truth.

You have a few options. You can go to family events with the expectation that you will be present only a short time and will stay superficial while you're there. If you want to keep that connection, then put in an appearance, say hello to everyone, and have a reason to leave after a short stay. If things go well, you can stay longer. When the old patterns begin, it's time to leave. If you choose this option, you have to go expecting your family to behave as they always do. Clearly tell them what behaviors will force your leaving. Then leave if any of those behaviors begin.

If you choose not to go at all, then find other ways to connect with your family—a short phone call, a note, a card. Tell your mom ahead of time that you will hang up the phone if things get ugly.

Continue to pray for your family and forgive them when they wrong you. According to the words of Jesus, this is an ongoing process. Ask God to help you respond as Christ would, using Matthew 5:44 as your guide. This is probably one of the hardest verses to put into practice. Jesus's words are radical: "But I say to you, love your enemies, bless those who curse you, do good to those who hate you, and pray for those who spitefully use you and persecute you" (NKJV).

Applying this verse doesn't mean you shouldn't set boundaries. On the contrary, make it clear what behavior drives you away. But remember the grace and mercy of God, that while we were yet sinners, He loved us and died for us. We didn't deserve His love. Maybe your family doesn't either, but with Christ in you, you are charged to love the unlovely. I'll be praying.

Dr. Linda

EXAMINE BIBLICAL GUIDELINES

Whenever you look for help regarding anger problems, it's important to examine biblical guidelines. God, the Creator of our human nature, knew we needed help in this area—lots of help! Therefore, He provided several biblical guidelines related to managing anger.[1]

Be quick to listen, slow to speak, slow to anger; resolve anger before the sun goes down (see James 1:19 and Ephesians 4:26). If we could follow this one guideline, most of us would see improvement in our relationships. It's difficult to listen and not become defensive when you're angry. Be ready to listen and commit to dealing with anger immediately. If you can't deal with it immediately, then set aside a time when you can. The point is to not let anger fester and become destructive to the relationship. If you are feeling so angry that you can't be "slow to anger," schedule a later time to deal with the problem. You may need time to calm down first.

Don't give full vent to your anger (see Proverbs 29:11). When you feel angry, it is your reaction that counts. Scripture tells us to exercise self-control over our tongues and actions. Self-control is a fruit of the Spirit leaving little room for behaviors like cursing, hitting, breaking things, and intimidating others. We have to learn to restrain our instinctual response to anger.

Stop and think (see Proverbs 14:17; 15:1–2; 16:29). How many times have you regretted afterward what you said and did when you were angry? Allow yourself time to think, calm down, and line up your response according to Scripture. You may want to take a time-out, pray, and take a few deep breaths before you respond.

Don't get caught up in name-calling (see Matthew 5:22). It's easy to blame and call the other person names when we are angry, but it isn't Christlike behavior. Again, restrain your tongue.

Don't take revenge on a violator (see Romans 12:19; Hebrews 10:30). We live in a culture obsessed with revenge and lawsuits. The Lord says vengeance is His and He will repay it. Today, this idea is radical. In most cases, you won't have many people reinforcing your position to not seek revenge. Understand that it is God's place to judge others, not yours. You live by His standards.

Forgive those who anger you (see Matthew 6:14). Forgiveness is important because it is the key to preventing bitterness and to healing relationships. Forgive others because Christ has forgiven you. This applies even when your anger is justified. When Mom is wrong, you still have to forgive her. (Forgiveness and grace are discussed in more detail in chapter 9.)

Get to the source of your anger (see Psalm 139:23–24). What is it that makes you feel so angry? What are the triggers? Identify the source of your anger and practice new ways to respond.

Don't stay angry (see Colossians 3:8). Acknowledge your anger but release it and move on. It is not worth the physical and emotional fallout you'll experience if you don't let go.

Give the anger to God (see 1 Peter 5:7). I know this sounds like a cliché, but giving your burdens to God brings tremendous relief. He can handle your anger and any other emotion you carry. Give it to Him and ask Him to help you react with grace and mercy.

Don't take offense (Proverbs 12:16; 19:11). This doesn't mean you pretend offenses don't exist. It means that when you have an opportunity to be offended, decide not to take on the offense. This is an act of tremendous choice.

When possible, don't associate with angry people (see Proverbs 22:24). When we spend time with people who are angry, insulting, and negative, it tends to rub off on us. Surround yourself with those interested in "dropping the rope" and living their lives in the grace and mercy of God.

Gain control over a quick temper (see James 1:19 and Proverbs 14:17, 29; 16:32; 19:19). I don't have to tell you how much trouble a hot temper brings. If you have problems in this area, you already know this to be true. You may want to take an anger-management class or practice the anger-control strategies suggested in this chapter.

TECHNIQUES AND STRATEGIES FOR SELF-CONTROL

The apostle James instructed us not only to hear the Word but to do it. But *knowing* what the Bible has to say about anger doesn't mean you will successfully implement all of the above guidelines. Usually we need additional help with the *doing* part. Continue to pray for self-control and ask God to help you. Then practice the following techniques and strategies.

Cool-Down Techniques

Before we move into anger-management strategies, it's helpful to learn and practice cool-down techniques. These are simple tools you can do to stay calm. Practice is what makes them work.

Take a few deep breaths. The opposite of tension is relaxation. When angry, you want to try and relax your body. Take a few deep breaths very slowly and deliberately. Inhale through your nose and breathe in from your diaphragm. Then exhale slowly through either your mouth or nose. Do this several times until you feel calmer and more relaxed.

Count to ten. It may be a cliché, but it works by helping you break the habit of reacting impulsively and quickly. When anger mounts, stop. Count slowly to ten before you allow yourself to say or do anything. This little pause slows you down and gives you a chance to think.

Take a brief time-out. If you feel anger welling up inside, take a time-out by walking away and taking ten or twenty minutes to calm yourself down. During the time-out, practice deep breathing or other cool-down techniques. Once you're calm, go back to the person and tackle the issue again.

Picture a calming scene in your mind. Distract yourself from the angry moment and think about something calming, like an ocean or the mountains. Close your eyes and place yourself in that calm scene until you feel relaxed.

Pray and/or meditate. When you feel out of control, there's no better immediate help than prayer. Stop, close your eyes, and silently ask God for help. Pray for self-control. Pray for the other person and the situation, and for God to move within it. Don't forget, His presence is always with you.

Deep muscle relaxation. When you feel your body going tense from anger, remove yourself from the situation and practice deep muscle relaxation. With practice, you can apply this to any situation in which you become angry. All you do is tense and hold a muscle group, then relax it and move on to another muscle group. For example, tense your right arm, holding your hand in a fist for ten seconds, then relax it. As you practice this with all your muscle groups, you teach your body to physically relax on your cue. Then, when you are in a tense situation, you can actually "tell" your body to do this. There are commercial audiotapes that walk you through each of the muscle groups. I recommend people practice this technique at night before bed and in the mornings.

What you don't want to do when you are angry is become aggressive. For years, people thought if they punched something, yelled, screamed, or threw things, these actions would release anger. Research shows that they don't release anger at all—and actually increase it.[2]

Anger-Management Strategies

After you have learned and practiced some cool-down strategies, you will have tools to use when anger wells up inside of you. Use those cool-down strategies to relax your body from the tension you feel when anger rises. Next, work on ways to *manage* your anger so you don't find yourself in constant need of trying to calm your body. These management strategies will help you feel less angry overall.

Avoid the nonessential triggers. One strategy is to simply avoid those triggers that are not essential to your relationship. For example, if you get in an argument every time you discuss movies with your mom, avoid the topic. Your opinion about movies is not *essential* in your relationship. In other words, you can have a relationship with your mom without discussing the latest movie. You might say something like, "Mom, it seems like every time we talk about movies, we fight. Let's talk about something else." Or just change the subject and avoid the anger trigger.

Some daughters choose not to ask their mom for advice because it ends in arguments. Others avoid discussing in-laws, finances, politics, religion, etc. If there is something insignificant that sets off anger and can be avoided without serious relationship fallout, try this strategy.

Stop the thoughts. If you have angry thoughts, refuse to keep thinking about them. When an angry thought comes into your head, silently yell, *Stop!* and redirect your thinking to something else. For example, if your mother tries to "guilt" you into coming for dinner and you think, *She always does this to me and wants to make me miserable,* mentally say, *Stop it. I'm not going there in my head.* This is the biblical equivalent of taking a thought captive. I tell my clients to reach out and grab the thought—capture it.

Change your thoughts. After you have stopped the thought, replace it with something more empathetic or positive. Use Philippians 4:8 as your guide. Think on things that are lovely, pure, true, noble, just, virtuous, praiseworthy, and admirable. Change your thought to something more positive: *Yes, she's driving me crazy, but I know she loves me,* for example.

Your thoughts influence your feelings, your feelings influence your perceptions, and your perceptions influence your thoughts. It's a repeating cycle. Changing your thoughts to something more loving and empathetic influences your angry feelings (decreases them), which then helps you perceive things more positively.

Get physical. Exercise, eating well, and getting enough sleep can both prevent stress from building up and serve as an outlet to release stress when it does occur. Pace yourself and try not to let yourself get bogged down with job-related responsibilities. When we are tired and out of sorts, we tend to be more irritable and edgy, and in that state we're more prone to "lose it" when a trigger occurs.

Establish fair-fighting rules. Your anger will be better managed if you establish fair-fighting rules beforehand. These are guidelines you and your mom need to follow when you're angry. The rules prohibit name-calling, swearing, belittling, physical contact, threats, yelling or screaming, use of drugs and alcohol, blame, and bringing up unrelated issues or issues related to the past. If either of you feels your anger is getting out of control, take a time-out or a longer break.

Practice being assertive. Anger can well up because we haven't asserted our needs or set boundaries. Before you storm off or decide the situation is hopeless, be assertive! Here's an example of a daughter who learned to be assertive. In therapy, Jessica told me her mother called her every night during dinner, and when she did, Jessica became very angry, silently fuming, *Why is she always calling and interrupting our family time? It makes me so mad that she does this. She isn't considering my feelings or wishes.*

"Jessica, does she even know your feelings or wishes?" I asked.

"I don't know, but she should!" Jessica replied. "She knows we eat dinner about the same time every night. She's just doing this to make me miserable."

"Look Jessica, *why* she does this is less important then having the phone calling stop. You need to be assertive and stop focusing on the *why*. If you really want to know why she does this, ask her and stop guessing at her motives. But asking her about it doesn't necessarily mean she will stop calling." I paused. "Tell me what you want to happen."

"I want her to stop calling me during dinnertime."

"OK, clear enough. Put that in the form of a request, then call and tell her."

Here's what Jessica said: "Mom, we eat dinner between six and seven o'clock every night. Because we consider that hour our family time, we won't be answering the telephone during dinner anymore. I wanted you to know so you wouldn't worry. So let's decide when a good time would be for both of us to talk on the phone."

Become empathetic. One thing that diffuses anger is empathy, the ability to see the world through your mother's eyes. We'll discuss the importance—and the how-to's—of developing empathy with your mom in the next chapter. For now, just try to see the big picture and put yourself in your mother's place.

Talk to friends. Women benefit tremendously from talking out their anger with a friend. A friend who listens, validates your concerns, and offers an objective view can help reduce anger.

Make an anger contract. If you are really struggling with your temper, make an anger contract. For every time you are calm and follow the fair-fighting rules, for example, reward yourself with something small. One client's system was to put money in a jar toward something she wanted to buy. Every time she "lost it," she withdrew money. Every time she managed her anger, she added to the stash.

Don't forget about humor. Remember our discussion about humor back in chapter 1? It goes a long way to discharge anger. Use it when you can.

Accept disagreement. If you are willing to accept the fact that disagreement with your mom is OK, you won't get angry so often. Expect disagreement.

Once you have a better handle on how to manage your anger or discharge it, practice what you've learned. Don't get discouraged if you don't make changes immediately. You are changing lifelong patterns and dealing with emotionally intense issues. If you lose control of your temper, apologize and try again. If you need to, go to a counselor or therapist for extra help. Do whatever it takes to manage your anger and not let it manage you.

Special Circumstances

Although I have focused on more general principles of dealing with anger, I do want to say a few words about adult daughters dealing with special circumstances. I can't begin to do justice to these topics in one chapter. Entire books have been dedicated to helping women and men deal with these issues. But I do want to note that in some circumstances, a daughter's reaction of anger is normal and may require special attention.

Daughters of Neglect

You may be a daughter who experienced neglect or abandonment growing up. Anger can result. Such was the case with Lynne. When she came to me for therapy, she expressed the situation like this.

"Lynne, tell me about your mother."

"She was never there when I needed her."

"And how do you feel about that?"

"I remember crying myself to sleep, wishing she'd come home and take care of me."

"And how do you feel about that?"

"One time I waited by the window for hours because she promised to take me shopping. She never showed up that day."

"And how do you feel about that?"

"Why do you keep asking me the same question? How would you feel about that? I felt angry, and I still feel angry. In fact, I'm angry that you keep asking me that stupid question."

"Are you angry or hurt?"

"Hurt? Are you kidding? She's the one who never came through for me. She should feel bad. I feel angry."

"Does that anger make you feel powerful and strong?"

"I don't know. I never thought about it."

"Think about it."

"Yeah, I guess so. It sort of makes me feel in control. Like she can't hurt me."

"What does hurt feel like?"

"Hurt? I don't want to feel hurt. When you hurt, you are weak and vulnerable. I prefer anger."

"Do you think anger is a cover for the hurt you feel?"

"Maybe, but let's not go there. I need to be angry with my mom or I might start to cry and never stop."

Lynne was angry. Her memories of childhood consist of an absent mom who spent most of her days and nights with different men. When Lynne's mom was present, she made many promises she never fulfilled.

Under Lynne's anger hid a hurt little girl who had never grieved the loss of her mom through neglect. Staying angry allowed Lynne to avoid the sadness that she believed would overwhelm her. Feeling the sadness was just as important as feeling the anger. Both were needed in order to help Lynne grieve the loss. Ironically, Lynne's anger also helped her feel connected to her mom.

Lynne was frightened by the enormity of emotion that was inside her. It felt like a dam would break if she gave up the anger and acknowledged the hurt. She feared the flood of emotion that would ensue. Because of this fear, she remained defensive against the hurt. Anger was her defense. Would she fall apart and never recover if she faced the depth of her wound? She wasn't sure.

Lynne's anger was based in reality. Her childhood would never be relived with a mom who chose her over strange men. This was a tremendous loss that needed to be acknowledged and grieved. But part of that grieving process required her to move out of the anger and visit the hurt. It's not that her anger was wrong. It wasn't, given her experience. But holding on to that anger as a protective cover prevented her from feeling the deep hurt. She was emotionally stuck. Facing the pain without anger would be intense, but she could survive it.

If you've suffered a history of mother neglect, find a caring therapist who will help you face the pain of that experience. The solution is not to stay angry but to release that anger and give way to the hurt. Even though it will be painful, it will help you heal from the pain of the past.

Daughters of Abuse

Many of you reading this have been the target of out-of-control anger. You've been physically and emotionally beaten, verbally degraded, and the victim of violent tempers. Or perhaps you've experienced an unthinkable betrayal and violation such as sexual abuse by a mother.

Anger is a normal reaction for a daughter who has been abused. Emotions of childhood trauma include terror, rage, denial and numbing, unresolved grief and shame, and guilt. When mother-daughter incest enters the picture, there is a major disturbance in the daughter's nurturing and dependency needs. In these cases, daughters need a safe, therapeutic environment to heal. Part of the healing process requires moving through the anger involved. Usually, work with a professional therapist is recommended.

One of the fallouts of suffering abuse is getting stuck in the emotion of anger and bitterness. Even though you have every right to feel angry, you can't heal while you stay in that angry place. And the toll the anger takes on your physical and emotional health is immense.

If you're dealing with both abuse and neglect, empathy (the focus of the next chapter) can help you try to understand why your mother did what she did. This understanding doesn't excuse the horror you experienced, and it won't remove the pain or cause you to forget, but it may provide a context for the betrayal.

Women often ask if they have to confront abuse in order to get better. This is a decision that should be made prayerfully and with the guidance of a professional therapist trained to treat abuse and neglect. Every situation is so individual that it needs careful thought and planning. In many cases, confronting abuse does not end with the abuser taking responsibility for her actions. Thus, you will need to be prepared for this. Talk to a trained professional and do what's necessary to move through the healing process.

Daughters of Divorce

Anger and hurt are felt when one's parents divorce. If you are a child of divorced parents, you may have developed an appreciation for the complexities of love and intimate relationships as you grew into adulthood. However, there may still be many unresolved issues related to your parents' divorce, and those hurts and feelings of anger can feel fresh for a long, long time.

When divorce occurs during a daughter's adolescence, the normal tensions of this developmental stage can be impacted for the daughter. Watching her mom hurt and then trying to deal with her own feelings of anger can create a wrench in the daughter's own separation process. She may worry about her mom, side with her, stop pushing for her own independence, comfort her mom, or feel responsible not to put any more pressure on Mom, given her emotional state. Daughters see the vulnerability, the tears, the heartache, the anger, and they can't make it better.

Mothers and daughters can grow closer following a divorce. Usually this happens when daughters are able to address their anger over the divorce—anger at either or both parents for not making the marriage work, anger at the breaking up of the family unit, anger at the loss of income and resources, anger at the loss of the physical presence of both parents, anger at losing a model for making love and intimacy work, anger at behaviors that may have contributed to the breakup such as affairs, gambling, addictions, or poor financial planning. The resulting anger can be a huge burden and needs to be addressed.

Anger is a normal reaction to all the loss experienced with divorce. If you and your mother have not talked through your reactions and you still feel angry over your parents' divorce, schedule a time to do that. You should also do the same with your father. It doesn't matter how old you are now, this step will help you deal more effectively with your anger. The purpose is for you to confront your anger, not blame your parents. If your parents are unwilling to help you or listen, find a support group or therapist who's willing to walk you through the losses.

Daughters of Addiction

If you are a daughter who grew up with a mom who struggled with substance abuse, you have anger! Your mom's altered state and time spent with the bottle or drugs meant there was less of her for you. The impact of drugs and alcohol on her functioning and her personality resulted in more losses for you as a daughter.

In his helpful book *Families Under the Influence*, psychotherapist Michael Elkin says, "Alcoholics explore the dark side of self for all of us. They therefore provide us with a unique opportunity to practice love and forgiveness."[3] Part of forgiveness, as we will learn in chapter 9, requires us to release our anger toward and judgment of those who have hurt us or let us down. Daughters of alcoholics have been disappointed many times over. It is critical to work through the resulting anger.

NO MATTER THE CAUSE OF YOUR ANGER at your mother, your job is to not let that anger dominate your life and control you. Anger leads to bitterness, and bitterness is a dark place to live. Do what you can to release your anger, to manage and control it. You may be the one who has to let go first. Whether or not your mother responds in kind, you will benefit by responding in a godly way to trials and difficulties that are often the precursors for anger. In the words of the psalmist:

Be angry, and do not sin.
Meditate within your heart on your bed, and be still. Selah[4]

THOUGHT POINTS

1. What is the role of anger in your relationship with your mother? Is your anger normal? Healthy? Damaging? On a scale from one to ten, rate the anger level in your relationship with your mother. Is anger a problem between the two of you?

2. What things trigger anger in either of you?

3. Examine the biblical guidelines given. How well do you do at following them?

4. If you have problems with anger, consider which cool-down techniques may help you.

5. Practice the anger-management strategies outlined in this chapter and continually assess how well they're working. Consider what still needs to change and how you can make those changes.

6. If you are a daughter of any of the special circumstances mentioned and you are unable to make progress in improving your relationship with your mom in these areas, consider the possibility of therapy.

EMPATHY: SEEING THE BIGGER PICTURE

I'M A LOUSY PHOTOGRAPHER. The people in my photographs usually have red eyes and cropped-off heads and tend to be out of focus. It's depressing. But despite my lack of skill or talent, I still keep clicking away.

On a recent trip to the Napa Valley in northern California, I stayed at a fabulous inn surrounded by beautiful vineyards. The vistas from my windows were spectacular. Hoping to capture some of the beauty of the region, I took several photographs of the countryside. When the photos were developed, they showed only small sections of the landscape, hardly capturing the splendor I had experienced in person. I was so disappointed.

As I stood staring at my camera (thinking it was the enemy), I noticed there was a panoramic-view button on it. Even though I had owned the camera for a while I had never noticed this option and never bothered to read the operating instructions. Had I used the wider lens, I would have captured more of the scenery. The panoramic-view button was there to help me, but I never saw it.

SEEING THE BIG PICTURE

Daughters can be like inexperienced photographers. Sometimes we have trouble seeing the big picture when it comes to dealing with our mom. We tend to see only a narrow snapshot of Mom's life, just the part that involves us. We forget that Mom is a complex woman shaped by many forces. It is my hope that after you read this chapter, you will think differently about your mother—that your view of her will be expanded.

In order to go home again and make peace with your mother, you need to understand some of the complexities that influence her life. When you do, your relationship with her will improve. If you choose to see her from only your limited perspective (your regular lens), you'll be disappointed and often confused.

Do you ever throw up your hands and say, "My mother! I just don't get her."

Well, chances are you *don't* "get" her. So often we are too busy thinking about our own problems that we rarely consider life from Mom's vantage point. Yet learning to do so could help us; it is critical to our growth as adult daughters.

Perhaps a spiritual analogy will help. When you first come to know God, you are happy and amazed at what God does for you. He saved you, put His Spirit in you, and gave you His Living Word. In the beginning of your relationship, you tended to focus on what God does for you, how He changes you, how He meets your needs and loves you. It's all about what God does for you.

The deeper you go in this relationship and the more you mature as a believer, the less you focus on your needs and the more you focus on who God is. You study and read all about Him, His promises, His character, His actions, and His love. You hunger for more. And the more intimate you become in your relationship with Him, the more you realize the complexities and mysteries of God. Yet He is still personal and available to you. Through this growing intimacy, some of His mysteries are revealed, and you understand more about His character.

One of the rewards of knowing God intimately is learning to see the world through His eyes. What an incredible gift this is! It's like putting a new lens on the camera of your life, one with greater clarity and wisdom. It lets you see that, although we are all imperfect, we are human beings created in the image of God and loved by Him unconditionally.

The same progression can happen with you and your mother. When you were a child, it was all about you and what you needed. But as you grow and mature, your focus changes. Most daughters long to know more about their mother—what her life was like as a child, how she was influenced by her generation, what dreams and goals she had that may have gone unrealized. The more you know about her life, the more you are able to see her as a complex person, not just as a mom who doesn't always act the way you want her to act. In other words, you need to get to know her on a more adult basis. Amazingly, you'll find that the more you discover about her, the more you discover about yourself.

In order to develop a deeper intimacy with your mom, turn on your panoramic-view button. Widen your lens. Consider whether the influences that shaped her life also impact yours. And think about how those influences affect your relationship.

THE WIDER LENS OF EMPATHY

Empathy is a necessary ingredient in any healthy relationship, but it is especially important when you reach adulthood and deal with your mother. When you're an adult, it's time to stop seeing the world through child eyes and learn to appreciate your mom's adult struggles. What motivates her to act the way she does? If you get to know her better, you may be able to answer that question.

Empathy simply means really "seeing" your mom, getting to know her in an in-depth way that enables you to put yourself in her shoes in order to better understand her. To carry the "lens" analogy a bit further, empathy means seeing the world through her eyes. Wow! Wouldn't *that* change the way the two of you relate?

Here's an example. Karen was embarrassed to go to restaurants with her mother. At the end of each meal, her mother always asked for a doggy bag and loaded everything left from the meal into the bag. Karen was embarrassed by this behavior and repeatedly asked her mother to not do it. But the behavior continued.

One night when Karen and her mom were leaving a nice restaurant, Karen sat in the car and angrily confronted her mom. "I've told you over and over to stop taking food home from the restaurant when you're with me. You embarrass me when you do this. Can't you stop making me feel so uncomfortable? I don't even want to be seen with you when you do this."

Stunned, her mother sat in silence. "Karen, when I take food home, it has nothing to do with you. I remember going hungry many times when I was a girl. My mother taught me to be grateful for whatever food we had at any given meal and to never waste food. Since we paid for the food at the restaurant, I didn't want it to go to waste. That's all. I figure the restaurant will throw it out anyway. I wasn't trying to make you feel bad. I never understood why this bothered you so. I guess I still don't."

"It just looks cheap to me, like we are low class or something," Karen answered. "Or like you are some homeless person who can't afford to eat out."

"Well, I do save where I can. I'm on a fixed budget and try to be frugal. I don't have much income, you know. Since your father died, I worry about my finances. Sometimes I think about my childhood days of hunger," her mother replied.

Karen suddenly saw her mother through the panoramic lens. "I'm sorry I got so angry over this," she said. "I never really thought about it, especially given your childhood and all. I was only concerned that you were making me look bad. I never considered your point of view or even thought to ask you about it. I just got mad because I thought it made me look bad. I have no idea what it's like to be hungry or to be uncertain about my next meal. And I've never dealt with being on a fixed income."

Karen realized she didn't understand her mom very well but was quick to yell at her. She would never take food home in a doggy bag herself, but then she also hadn't grown up hungry and scraping for every bite. Now she knew that her mother's behavior was motivated by childhood poverty, not by trying to embarrass her daughter. When Karen realized what motivated her mom, she became more empathetic and less angry. Her mom's behavior made more sense, and she realized it wasn't aimed at irritating her.

Karen's mom hadn't understood why her daughter became so angry. Sometimes it seemed that all Karen ever did was yell at her. When she heard how embarrassed Karen felt about her doggy bags, she offered to stop taking food from restaurants since it obviously bothered her so.

As a result of this brief interaction, Karen invited her mom to tell her more about her childhood, a topic they had rarely discussed. Karen realized she had judged her mom unfairly; she hadn't known about the trauma her mom experienced as a child. Karen's willingness to widen her lens brought the two of them closer.

Why Do I Have to Change?

You may be reading this and thinking, *Well, good for Karen, but I'm not making the first move. Why do I have to be the one to change? You don't know the number of times my mother has hurt me. Why should I try to understand her when she doesn't bother trying to understand me?*

Throughout this book, I will be challenging you as a daughter to make the first move in correcting or improving your relationship with your mother. After years of counseling women, I have concluded that you can wait forever for your mother to make a move toward you—or you can take a risk and make a move toward her. Relationships involve taking risks and making changes. Only children argue about who goes first!

Maybe it feels unnatural or uncomfortable to make changes. But if you want a better relationship with your mom, you'll have to learn to tolerate being "uncomfortable" for a while. People often stay stuck in their old patterns of relating, simply because they don't want to feel uncomfortable. As weird as it sounds, people would prefer to keep on doing what's familiar, even when it obviously isn't healthy.

If you choose to respond in a new way, you will change your relationship. Remember the rule: a change in one person's behavior causes a change in the other.

Learning to Be More Empathetic

People often ask if empathy can be learned. The answer is yes. You may have to work hard at developing this skill, but with practice you can learn it.

Developing empathy is important because people are more willing to change when they feel understood or heard. Just think about the example above with Karen and her mother. A little understanding went a long way to make things better. Think about it.

Aren't you more likely to change when you feel understood? Your mother is no different. Your efforts to acknowledge her struggles and put yourself in her place will be rewarded. She will most likely be willing to share her heart more readily.

LESS JUDGMENT, MORE UNDERSTANDING

Empathy involves a nonjudgmental attitude. It requires some awareness that people act the way they do for various reasons. Let's face it: daughters are good at judging Mom. A nonjudgmental attitude requires you to suspend your opinion for a moment and try to hear hers. Then, if you are bothered by what you hear, you can still make choices not to agree with her or live by her rules. But at least you've heard her and understand the backdrop of her life.

Let me share another example. Heidi and her mother, Lisa, rarely spoke. When they did, Lisa usually wanted something from Heidi. Now Lisa wanted to talk to Heidi, but Heidi suspected her mother's only reason for contacting her was because Lisa's mother had died, and now Heidi was about to inherit some money from her grandmother.

Lisa had been drunk and emotionally unavailable most of Heidi's life—just like her own mother had been. During Lisa's childhood her mother spent most of her days asleep on the couch. Lisa had basically raised herself. When Lisa was a teenager, she was raped by a neighbor while her mom lay drunk in the next room. From that point on, Lisa also began to drink heavily. The generational pattern was repeating. Grammy had been emotionally absent from Lisa, and now Lisa was emotionally absent from Heidi.

Because of the influence of a caring teacher who mentored Heidi through high school, Heidi was sober. She was also determined not to deal with her emotional pain by numbing herself through alcohol.

She desperately wanted her mom to sober up and have a relationship with her. But there seemed to be no movement in that direction.

Now Lisa had contacted her, wanting to talk. Confused and upset, Heidi wanted to know how to talk to her mom about Grammy's death. In therapy we discussed the importance of empathy, and when Heidi returned her mother's phone call, she began like this: "Mom, I'm sorry Grammy died. I know you didn't ever get to know her well. I feel sad about that. I know she wasn't there for you when you needed her. And now she's gone. How are you doing with her death?"

Heidi's mom began to cry. She was surprised by what Heidi said. No one ever asked how she was feeling. Mostly they just got angry with her for drinking. "I'm not doing too well with it," she answered. "I feel guilty and pretty mixed up. I have been drinking a lot. It hurts too much."

"I'm hurting, too, and I don't have anyone to talk to either," Heidi told her mother. "But I found a therapist who will listen. I know how you feel about being alone and all, but Mom, I don't want to cover up my feelings by drinking. Will you ever face your life without the alcohol?"

Her mother grew silent and then said, "I haven't made it easy for you, have I? But, Heidi, I really don't know how to face this kind of stuff. I'm a screwup. All I know how to do is drink the pain away, and I don't want you to be like me so I stay away."

Heidi calmly replied, "Mom, you know people would help you if you would let them. Someone helped me. That's why I don't drink. I would like to know you better, but the alcohol gets in our way. Remember how you hated it when your mother drank? How alone and lost you felt? It's keeping us apart. But whenever you're ready to try, I'm here. I'd like to have you in my life."

She hung up the phone and began to cry. Her mother's decision to avoid pain and not get help hurt. It was a loss Heidi faced daily. But Heidi's understanding of the generational pattern between mothers and daughters in her family helped her be less angry. And she was able to have empathy for her mother despite her mom's bad choices.

Understanding her mother's life of addiction, sexual abuse, and pain helped keep Heidi's heart soft toward her mother. The empathy she gave her mother didn't mean she ignored the reality of their problems. Nor did it mean she approved of her mother's drinking. She didn't. But empathy helped keep the door open for change.

To my knowledge, Heidi's mother never chose sobriety, but because Heidi remained empathetic toward her mother, she didn't live with constant anger and resentment. She had every reason to feel both, but she chose a higher path. Had a teacher not intervened in her life, Heidi might be drinking now too. She considered it God's grace that she had been rescued. She knew that same grace was available for her mother.

Heidi understood her mom's pain. It was similar to her own. But Heidi made different choices. She hopes her mom will choose to change someday as well. Until then, empathy allows Heidi to remain connected to her mom.

LISTEN

If you want to develop empathy for your mom, listen to what she says about her life. After you've listened, repeat back what you've heard to show that you understand her feelings. Then ask her if what you said and heard were accurate. If she gives you the thumbs-up, you are on your way to a more productive relationship.

Daughters need to practice listening more. Instead of always thinking about how we feel or how we will respond, we need to hear our mother's point of view. We may not always agree with her position, but we can at least try to understand it.

In my relationship with my mother, I've tried to argue my point less and learn more about hers. She comes from a different generation and has been impacted by different experiences than I have. She was a middle daughter of eight children; I am the youngest and only daughter of three. She is living through a stage of life I've yet to experience. All these variations make for a difference in perspective. I need to be willing to hear her perspective.

Yes, it took me awhile to get to this place because of the intense feelings that seem to naturally exist between mothers and daughters. But I've learned that our relationship is more rewarding when it's less about my being right and more about our communicating. As a therapist, I know that everyone communicates better when he or she feels understood. I work very hard at listening to my clients. The least I can do is offer that same courtesy to my mom.

In dealing with my own mom, sometimes I'm right and sometimes she is. Empathy isn't about winning arguments (see the next chapter on resolving conflict). It's about developing a skill that sets the stage for better communication and understanding.

Every Mom Has Worth

Empathy also assumes that your mom has worth. Maybe she is alcoholic like Heidi's mother, depressed, and critical; maybe she has a history of sexually acting out and making bad choices. It doesn't matter. She has worth just because she was born. Even if she's yet to discover her own worth, you can treat her as one who is valued. Worth is not determined by what we do or don't do. We are valuable simply because we are created by God.

If you can remind yourself of this, it helps. In problematic mother-daughter relationships, it sometimes helps daughters to think about what their mother might have been like if she had been given unconditional love and acceptance as a child by her parents or by her spouse. Would it change how she acted? Most agree it would.

As daughters review their mom's history, it's usually easy to see if those basic relationship ingredients—love and acceptance—were missing. If they were, no wonder their mom had trouble giving love and acceptance to them. Mom never received love and acceptance herself! Knowing this doesn't erase your pain, but it helps you make sense out of the situation.

In Susie's case, this understanding was the answer to her marital problems. Susie came to therapy because she was compulsively overeating and pushing her husband away. Susie's husband didn't know how to help. When he tried, she just got angry and seemed to eat more.

Susie felt out of control. As we explored what was happening, Susie recalled a similar out-of-control feeling with her mother when Susie was growing up. According to her account, she tried desperately to please her mom but felt it was a losing battle and started to rebel. Her rebellion only confirmed her mother's criticism. Susie felt trapped and unloved. Nothing she did seemed to win her mother's approval.

Susie realized that this same dynamic was playing itself out in her relationship with her husband. She was testing him to see if he would accept her unconditionally. Would he love her if she was fat?

But the real issue wasn't her weight. She worried that her husband would reject her if she wasn't perfect. Realizing that the root of her problem was with her mother and not her husband, Susie began to work on that relationship. Mainly she had to let go of the wish to have her mother's approval. It was a loss she needed to grieve. When she did, she no longer needed to test her husband, and she stopped overeating.

R-E-S-P-E-C-T

Respect is important to any relationship. At the least, you can respect your mother for giving you life. Honoring your mother and your father is a commandment, not an option. If you obey this commandment, God will honor you.

I understand that respect is often earned and that some of your mothers may not have earned your respect. I'm not asking you to manufacture something that isn't there. I'm simply suggesting that you can give respect for the position of motherhood. For some, that may be all you can do. For others, there may be much more on which to build.

WARMTH

The more you can approach any conversation with your mom with the same warmth you would give a friend, the further you'll go in coming together. It amazes me how often daughters scream and yell at their mother; these are behaviors they would never do in other relationships. Once when I was a teenager, I had an argument with my mom and actually threw a phone at her! If I did that to one of my friends, she would never speak to me again!

BE CONCRETE

Talk to your mom in specific terms and not just vague generalizations. Rather than saying, "Mom, I love you" (which is a good thing but could be even more expressive), try being more specific: "Mom, I love it when you call and check on me" or "talk to the grandkids" or "offer to baby-sit" or "give me your smile of approval."

Again, everyone likes to hear specifically what he or she does right—and needs to hear specifically what the problem may be. If you say, "You are so difficult!" and storm off, it's hard to know what you are reacting to. But if you say, "I get upset when you call me irresponsible," the communication is clear. Concrete communication is better than vague generalizations.

WIDENING YOUR LENS FURTHER

As you work on being more empathetic, your picture of your mom will expand. Try to identify the unique influences that comprise her life. Your mother, like you, doesn't live in isolation. Her world is made up of more than just your relationship (this may come as a shock to some of you). In addition to her family life, her world is shaped by the generation in which she was reared, her sibling position in her family of origin, her race, ethnicity, social class, religion, and even the part of the country where she grew up.

The same is true for you. You are more than your mother's daughter. You are a woman shaped by multiple influences. And these influences impact your relationships as well as your thoughts about what it means to function in this world as a woman and a daughter.

If you want to make peace with your mom or improve your relationship, identify the influences that have made her the woman she is today. Here are some places to begin.

Different Ages, Different Generations

Mothers and daughters come from two different generations. This means their ideas about being female may differ and clash. For example, I was influenced by the women's movement that swept our country when I was a young woman about to embark on my college education. When I applied to the University of Michigan's pre-law program as a high school senior in the 1970s, the cultural message was that women could be anything they wanted to be. I wanted to be a lawyer.

My mother grew up in a time when women had few professional options. So when I was ready to begin college, she had concerns about my making it in a field she saw dominated by men. The only lawyers we knew were male and were often perceived as ruthless, not a feminine quality. My mother had doubts about the viability of a legal career for her daughter, and she shared those concerns with me. Her opinion was based on her own experiences of being a business-woman in a man's world during her generation. Of course, at the time I thought she was being controlling and trying to limit my options. I had no understanding of her life experiences and how they related to my choice of career.

Obviously, I didn't become a lawyer. But when I understood her point of view, I saw her as being protective, not controlling. Consequently, my reaction was much more positive.

Today, I wouldn't even blink if my daughter said she wanted to pursue law. It's a different generation. Times have changed. I have women friends who are lawyers and don't see this profession defined by gender. While there are still more male than female lawyers, women have acceptance in the field. The only concern I have about law school is how to pay for it!

Women have experienced radical changes in the last century in America. Just think about the last four decades alone. The 1960s were strongly influenced by the second wave of feminism. The 1970s gave rise to unisex fashion, soon to be replaced by the 1980s image of the tough working girl dressed in a suit. In the 1990s, the third wave of feminism preached "girl power." The mantra was that women no longer needed to be like men to be successful. They had power in their own right.

Mothers and daughters are shaped by these generational forces.

Understanding generational differences is important to keeping your relationship strong. What was thought to be the mark of femininity in one generation may change in the next. Thus, there is a great need for dialogue and listening between mothers and daughters.

Alex, I'll Take Geography for $20

Have you ever thought about the influence of geography on your mother-daughter relationship? I never did until I moved from one part of the country to another.

The first time I moved to the South from the North, I was repeatedly told by my southern coworkers to be less aggressive and less direct. In the South, I was told, women were supposed to be much more demure and passive. Well, passivity is not a trait for which I am known and one I didn't find particularly useful in the workplace up north. Now I had a problem. I had a northern mind housed in a southern body!

I had no role model for how to be a southern businesswoman. My mother worked all her life in the North where women were direct and assertive on the job. We didn't mince words; we got to the point. We identified the problem. Time is money. Life in the North moves fast, and you have to move with it. I was unprepared for this new environment, having been raised in the North by a working mother.

I had to adjust my way of doing things in order to fit into my new cultural climate. I often felt like it took too long to get projects moving—there was too much discussion, and we were wasting time—but I understood that the people around me did things differently. The North wasn't better, just different.

Today we live in such a mobile society that people from different geographical areas intersect more often. Just think of all the daughters of divorce who live in one part of the country, visit another, and

65

have to try and work under the expectations of a mom and stepmom who may live in different regions of the country with different expectations for daughters. Relationship strain can result if geographical differences are not recognized or discussed.

Not only are there geographical rules about relationships but there are also unspoken influences related to the color of your skin, the amount of money you make, and your ethnic background. All these things influence the way mothers and daughters interact.

Ethnicity, Class, and Race

How many of you laughed at the ethnic struggles Toula encountered in the movie comedy *My Big Fat Greek Wedding*? I laughed because the movie was funny but also because I could relate to the ethnic messages. I am not Greek, but every ethnic group has its own set of expectations that governs relationships. I am German. I'll never forget my father telling me that he could judge the worth of any young man who dated me by how clean his car was. If he had a messy car, beware!

In Toula's case, Greek girls were to marry Greek boys, have Greek babies, and cook a lot of Greek food. If she didn't marry, she was expected to work in the family business. Toula wanted something different for her life but was afraid to tell her family. When her dreams clashed with her Greek family's expectations, the fun began. She was forced to choose between the family's expectations and her own ideas, which often differed from the expectations for Greek women. The movie is a great example of how ethnicity influences mother-daughter relationships. It also shows an empathetic mother who realizes her Americanized daughter is from a different generation.

Here's another example from my own life. It may help you consider how you are influenced in your day-to-day life. Sometimes those influences are easy to see; other times they're not.

I grew up in a middle-class, German-American home. As an adult, I am faced with a related ethnic dilemma every week. It involves cleaning my house. I never seem to have time for housework but hate living in a dirty house. Can anyone relate? Balancing my time to clean, be with my family, and do my business-related work is quite a challenge. And how I manage it has everything to do with how I was trained to be a mother by my mother.

Cleanliness is next to godliness in the German family in which I was reared. A messy house is a sign of failure as a woman. After all, my mother worked a full-time job, kept an immaculate house (we could probably eat off the floors), attended every activity my two brothers and I ever participated in, and was a good wife to my dad. I don't know how she did it without being exhausted every night of her life. And remember, she didn't own a microwave!

The unspoken message was clear: women are expected to keep up with their business commitments and their households and their families. You did not sacrifice a clean house for any reason. And I don't care how sick you are, you will have on clean underwear when going to the hospital! As a child, I remember breaking my collarbone when I tripped while playing tag in the backyard. Before we went to the hospital for x-rays, my mom insisted on changing my shirt to a clean one. Arrgh! I still feel the pain of lifting my arm in and out of that sleeve! But I was clean for the doctor!

I try to use my PhD brain to tell me it's OK not to starch my husband's shirts or iron clothes perfect enough for military inspection. But I still feel the pressure and probably always will. Look, I'm not on antidepressants because of this. And it's not an issue with my mom. But it's an ingrained ethnic message that makes me a little nuts some days. And it certainly influences my thoughts about my role as a mother and daughter.

My friends, of course, have the solution. They want me to hire a housekeeper. Actually, I could afford to do so, but that's not the reason I don't. Hard work is also a German virtue! You shouldn't pay someone for work you can do yourself! And the one time I hired some Eastern European ladies to help me clean, I couldn't stop pitching in. It was like dusting with Grandma! So I was paying people while I worked alongside them. And besides, it bothered me to see these little old ladies work so hard. In a German family, you respect your elders and allow them to rest. By the time we were finished with coffee breaks, snacks, and my telling them to skip the hard part and then listening to the woes of their lives, it really wasn't worth the effort.

So I'm back to cleaning toilets and dealing with my ethnic angst!

Race and social class matter as well. For example, African American mother-daughter relationships have to contend with a collective history of injustice and slavery. Because of this history, family therapists have noted that an African American mother may teach her daughter that being a woman is all about developing survival skills, a message not heard by a white daughter in the suburbs.

In the best-selling novel *The Joy Luck Club*, Amy Tan explores the relationships between mothers and daughters of Chinese descent. The mothers, born in China before the 1949 revolution, watch with dismay as their Chinese-American daughters try their best to become Americanized. It is a touching story that highlights the mistreatment of one generation of Chinese women and how their experiences affect their relationship with their American-born daughters, who must deal with feelings of resentment regarding their nationality as they try to conform to American social pressures.

Not only does race impact mother-daughter relationships, but so does social class. Women in poverty situations typically contend with more social problems and have fewer resources than those in higher economic classes. One homeless woman's dream for her daughter was to find her a home, a place to live off the streets. In stark contrast, women with wealth make the choice of how many homes to own! Poverty impacts dreams and expectations. Wealth opens up options.

While it is not the purpose of this book to go into detail about how race, ethnicity, and class specifically influence mother-daughter pairs, I do want you to be aware that all these factors are a part of our collective lives and do influence our relationships. If you understand more about each of these areas, you can be more empathetic. Taking this wider view will give you a bigger picture of your mother's life.

You may want to do more reading about the specific ethnic, racial, and class issues that relate to your mother-daughter relationship. The more you understand, the easier it is to look at your mother in context. Many conflicts arise because we fail to take the big picture into consideration. We don't consider the larger messages that may be influencing our decisions and actions.

You may be thinking, *This sounds too complicated and hard, as though I have to become a sociologist to better understand my mother.* You don't. Any discussion the two of you can generate in these areas will help. The more aware you are of these issues, the more empathetic you will likely become.

Religion

Religion is another cultural context in which families grow. I grew up in a Christian home and have adopted those Christian values as my own. Because my mother and I share the same Christian faith, we have a similar context in which to discuss our lives. This makes our relationship easier.

Problems come when mothers and daughters don't share common religious beliefs. Sharon was one of those daughters. Her mother's religious beliefs conflicted with hers over the role women were to have in the church. Her mother felt the only duties women could hold were more traditional—as nursery workers, in women's ministries, or in extending hospitality. The minister at the mother's church reinforced this belief from the pulpit.

When Sharon married, she and her husband attended a different church that allowed women to hold positions of spiritual authority. Sharon was elected a deacon and was very active. Her mother was upset by this, feeling Sharon shouldn't have such a position. Sharon stayed true to her belief, and it created a constant tension between the two women.

At first Sharon and her mom simply avoided the subject of women in the church. But one day Sharon asked her mother to explain her position more fully. She listened carefully as her mother explained how she had come to her conclusions. Then Sharon asked her mother to hear her position. At the end of the discussion, both women agreed to disagree on the subject of a woman's role in the church. They decided to agree on an essential: they both loved God. And hey, at least they were both in church. As a result of their being able to discuss the issue with empathy for each other, the tension between them decreased.

Listen and Learn

Cultural understanding is important. Our culture doesn't determine who we are, but it does influence our actions and relationships. If you want to better understand your mother, be empathetic and learn about the cultural forces that have shaped her life.

I'm really asking you to make a decision. Continuing our analogy of the camera, I'm asking you to choose which lens you will choose to view your mom. Do you want to see her as a small snapshot of a woman? There she is in your picture, alone, reaching out to you with no backdrop to frame her. Or will you choose the panoramic view, a woman surrounded by a background, vistas, and color? If you choose to widen your lens and see her as God does, fearfully and wonderfully made, you'll get that bigger picture.

For those of you determined to widen your lens, use the questions below to help you consider these important issues and think about how your and your mother's cultures impact the two of you. If it's possible to discuss these questions with your mother, please do. But don't be surprised if she hasn't thought about what it means to be middle class, Italian, white, or whatever. In the end, the information you consider should open some new doors of understanding.

THOUGHT POINTS

1. Have you ever thought to ask God to change your perspective, to help you see your mother through His eyes? Consider the way God sees both of you (for example, that you are beautifully and wonderfully made, His child, loved, justified, bought with a price, chosen, adopted, redeemed, one with Him in spirit). Think about how your relationship would change if you put on the eyes of Christ.

2. Compare the messages from your generation with those from your mother's generation in terms of being a woman, mother, or daughter. What differences do you think you both bring to your relationship because you've been raised in those different generations? Do those differences cause problems, or can they be positive?

3. Can you identify any racial, class, ethnic, religious, or geographical messages you may have received about being female? Think about how those messages play out in your relationship with your mom.

4. Are there any cultural messages you would like to change or that you find cause tensions between the two of you?

5. What strengths do you have because of the larger cultural groups you belong to?

6. Do these cultural messages feel restrictive or limiting? If so, how?

4

HANDLING CONFLICT

Y OU NEED TO PUT A HAT ON THAT BABY."

"Why? It's not that cold. She really doesn't need a hat."

"She'll get sick if she doesn't wear a hat and cover her ears. Babies get sick when the wind gets in their ears."

"Mom, that's ridiculous. Wind in the ears makes them sick?"

"Yes! Don't laugh. I always put a hat on you, and you didn't get sick."

"Well, I doubt that had anything to do with wind."

"Listen to your mother and put a hat on that baby."

Mother-daughter conflict! Can you relate? I'm reminded of Gilda Radner's character Rosanne Rosannadanna on *Saturday Night Live,* who used to complain, "It's always something."

When it comes to mothers and daughters, it's always something!

MOTHER-DAUGHTER CONFLICT IS NORMAL

"My mother and I are so much alike that we often butt heads."

"My mother and I have major differences, but we rarely talk about them."

"I just try to be a peacemaker. Doesn't the Bible tell us not to fight?"

"I feel so bad. I visit my mom and vow I won't argue with her, but I do."

"I just want to learn to get along with her better. Help!"

Have you ever made or thought any of the above statements? They come from adult daughters trying to sort out the complicated mother-daughter bond. Conflict is normal. You aren't pathological or ungodly if you have conflict. I often hear women of faith say that Christians shouldn't have conflict. Somehow conflict is wrong, they say, because Christ called us to be peacemakers.

Yes, Christ wants us to live in harmony and peace, but that doesn't mean we avoid conflict or pretend problems don't exist. In fact, Jesus was so concerned that we learn how to properly deal with one another that He specifically provided conflict guidelines.

Conflict is a part of every relationship, and it's usually driven by a *need*: I need your approval, agreement, permission, love, acceptance, appreciation, validation—I need *something*. That need can be met, or it can become an issue between two people.

Not only is conflict need-driven, but it surfaces when one person doesn't feel loved or desired. If you feel unloved or disconnected from your mother's life, that situation can be a source of hurt and conflict. The reverse may also occur: a mother may want more of her daughter's time than the daughter is willing to give. When the adult relationship between mother and daughter isn't negotiated in terms of time and expectations, or when it lacks a true intimate bond, both can feel left out and unloved.

You may be thinking, *My mother-daughter conflicts aren't about needs or feeling unloved. My mother just does things that bother me. It's her irritating traits and habits that cause our arguments and disagreements.*

Well, join the club. People we love or value tend to make us crazy at times because they don't always act the way we would like them to act. They have weird quirks or do things that annoy us. My daughter probably has a long list of irritants about me! And don't forget, we daughters can be annoying and irritating too. Remember, the acorn doesn't fall far from the tree!

Read the following comments from mothers and daughters and see if you can relate. These comments depict mothers and daughters struggling to deal with each other's annoying and irritating behaviors:

"I love my daughter, but she's too abrupt."

"My mother isn't sensitive to my time limitations."

"My daughter is too permissive as a parent. She gives in to her children."

"My mom cries too easily."

"My daughter doesn't call me enough."

"My mother is a hypochondriac."

"My daughter is late to every family event."

"My mother is a terrible cook."

"My daughter complains about her weight all the time."

OK, now it's your turn. Complete this sentence: "My mother . . ." The list of endings for that sentence can be long or short. The point is, we all *have* a list. Problems come when we try to change the other person. But remember, you can't change another person, only your response to that person.

Because mothers and daughters aren't clones of each other (well, at least not yet!), there *will* be differences. How we deal with those differences matters. We want to be able to solve conflicts when they arise. But while conflict in the mother-daughter relationship seems to be a natural occurrence, conflict *resolution* is not! It is a skill to be learned and practiced. And even then, it doesn't seem to be one that many of us do well. Too often our good intentions go out the window when the emotional heat rises.

A Daughter's Journey Home

In order to become good at conflict resolution, first deal with your emotional reactivity—the way you respond emotionally to your mother (see chapter 1). Then begin to sort out your differences with your mom. These fifteen questions will help you think more about how you and mom handle disagreements.

1. We agree on most things.
   Yes   No

2. We often argue.
   Yes   No

3. We resolve our arguments.
   Yes   No

4. One or both of us apologizes when we are wrong.
   Yes   No

5. We speak only when we have to speak to each other.
   Yes   No

6. We get angry at each other most times we are together.
   Yes   No

7. We compromise during arguments.
   Yes   No

8. We argue about small things.
   Yes   No

9. We stay upset with each other long after a disagreement.
   Yes   No

10. We bring up issues from the past when we argue.
    Yes   No

11. We call each other names.
    Yes   No

12. We become physical during an argument.
    Yes   No

13. One of us accommodates the other when a disagreement arises.
    Yes   No

14. We try to resolve problems when they occur.
    Yes   No

15. We usually end up solving our problem.
    Yes   No

If your answers show that you need help in handling your disagreements, keep reading! This chapter will help you learn healthy ways to resolve conflicts with your mom.

Underlying Tension

Researcher Karen Fingerman studied forty-eight pairs of elderly mothers and their midlife daughters and found that mothers and daughters can experience tension in their relationships without ever even confronting each other. Apparently about one-third of the moms and 40 percent of the daughters studied reported feeling negative with the other at least once a month.[1] Are any of us surprised by this, considering our shared histories and the numerous opportunities we have to engage in conflict and disagree? Where there is intimacy, there is usually tension.

Once we realize that it is normal to experience occasional annoyances or an ebb and flow of positive and negative feelings in our mother-daughter relationships, we also understand that existing tension may never be raised in the relationship. In fact, Fingerman went on to report that 81 percent of mothers and 60 percent of daughters in her study said they only deal with an open conflict once every few months or even less often.[2] So tension may be present and not acknowledged. What you do with that unacknowledged tension is up to you.

Does tension cause relationship problems for you? If so, it's time to deal with it and clear the air. As we learned in the last chapter, harboring bad feelings is not healthy for you nor productive for your relationship with your mother. It can cause you physical and emotional harm. Serious, ongoing conflict also damages relationships.

Conflict Styles Matter

Intimate relationships can sustain conflict and still survive it. If this wasn't true, none of us would survive a relationship! When conflict happens, the way you handle it can strengthen or hurt your relationship. Review these five broad and basic styles of handling conflict. Think about which one best describes you and which one best describes your mom.

Calm and rational. Of course, we'd all like to claim we use this style to settle disagreements—but we'd be lying. Some people are incredibly calm and rational when it comes to dealing with conflict. They listen well, offer support, are not defensive, show respect, and openly discuss a solution. They have a problem-solving style.

Fight and argue. If this is your style, when conflict appears, you yell, scream, call names, fight, or argue your way through the problem. Women with this style feel they must win every argument. They can be assertive or aggressive, but the style is definitely confrontational.

Avoid conflict. Maybe you are so uncomfortable with tension and dissent that you choose not to deal with problems when they emerge.

You hope problems go away, you're afraid to address the issue, or you hide behind the veil of being a peacemaker. Avoiders tend to believe that addressing relationship problems will damage the relationship or create even more problems. For them, it's better to pass over issues or deny they exist.

Compromise. Compromise, whether done aggressively or assertively, requires cooperation. People who compromise tend to believe there is more than one way to act or think about a situation. Usually women who compromise in dealing with their mother feel it is important to maintain a good relationship with her. They give a little and get a little in order to keep the relationship going smoothly.

Accommodate. Daughters who accommodate are agreeable—but usually at a cost to their personal selves. The general belief is that solving a conflict isn't worth risking relationship damage. It's better to accommodate and allow things to go smoothly.

Now here's the challenge: Once you identify your basic style of dealing with conflict, consider whether it's the same as your mother's style. If you both have different styles, conflict becomes more problematic.

Remember, just because you fight or avoid conflict doesn't mean your relationship is in trouble. If you and your mom solve conflict using similar styles, there are usually fewer problems. For example, if both of you are fighters, you may fight with each other but feel OK about fighting. This was the case with Terry and her mom. They used to have numerous arguments about Terry's choice of men. The two were constantly at each other's throat—but seemed to thrive in the relationship. When I asked how the fighting affected them, Terry told me, "We like to fight about these things. It helps both of us express our feelings and somehow we feel better afterwards." Her mother agreed. When I pointed out that not much seemed to change or get resolved, it didn't seem to matter to them.

With compatible ways of dealing with conflict, they were fine with their styles of interacting over differences. In fact, they tolerated each other's differences well. Terry also noted that her mother's point of view often influenced her behavior, even though she didn't acknowledge this fact during a disagreement.

Mothers and daughters seem to have more problems when their styles differ. Chris and her mom are a good example of this. Chris was a fighter and the one who usually raised issues in the family. Her mom was a conflict avoider and learned to keep problems to herself in her role as the dutiful wife and mother. Chris suspected that her mom wasn't being up-front about her true feelings because, although Chris was not making good choices and acting impulsively and angrily, her mom, who witnessed her inappropriate behavior regularly, never confronted her.

In therapy, Chris's mom admitted that her mother (Chris's grandmother) was a conflict avoider as well. The wife of an angry man, her mother learned to say little and stay out of his way. Chris's mom did the same. Her main style was conflict avoidance.

Chris's mom was afraid of her daughter's anger. It brought up painful memories about her dad. As a child, she had felt powerless to defend herself against his anger. When she experienced her daughter's anger, she reverted to that powerless state and became immobilized. So she avoided Chris when she acted in angry ways.

Chris sensed her mom's avoidance and confronted her. She valued her mother's opinion and wanted her to express it. With coaching, Chris's mom was able to tell Chris how uncomfortable she felt with her daughter's confrontational style. It triggered feelings from the past that led to her avoidance.

If Chris agreed to be less intense with confrontation, her mother said she would try to express her opinion when Chris asked. Both had to compromise their styles in order to accommodate the other. In this case, compromise and accommodation worked.

Mothers and daughters have amazing abilities to survive conflict and continue to love each other. However, conflict creates tension and stress, and the way you handle (or don't handle) that conflict can add to that tension and stress. So it helps to find acceptable ways to resolve conflict that will strengthen your intimate tie.

WHY SO MUCH CONFLICT?

In our teen years, family conflict actually strengthens our sense of self as we work out our identity. Think about it. We are trying to separate and become autonomous individuals. We are trying to find our voices. In that process, we will disagree and have different feelings and opinions than our mom and other members of our family. As we work through those differences, we learn how to deal with conflict and hold our own opinions and positions. Interacting with family is a great way to practice conflict-resolution skills. In fact, it's a primary teacher of conflict resolution—or the lack of it.

You may have grown up in a family that rarely resolved its problems. There was tension, stress, and conflict, but no one resolved the conflict. Family members may have numbed themselves from the problems through the use of substances, or they may have internalized the conflict and suffered depression, anxiety, or eating disorders, or lashed out in angry, destructive ways.

Not all family members are good models for conflict resolution. In fact, a bulk of my time in clinical practice is spent helping people learn to talk out problems and work through differences and disagreements. When you left home, you became a representative of whatever your experience was in your family as you grew up. Now the skills you learned in your family are put to the test at jobs, in marriages and friendships, and of course, in your family relationships.

Perhaps your family did teach good conflict-resolution skills, but, as daughters sometimes do, you chose to behave differently based on other influences. The unresolved emotional baggage you carry from your family, in addition to that picked up from other relationships and experiences, continues to impact your skill development as well.

In order to improve your mother-daughter relationship, solve problems, and reduce stress, learn to resolve conflict in healthy ways. No matter what happened in your past, clean up the problems between your mother and you as much as possible. If she isn't already, she may become a wonderful resource and support. If she already is a positive model of conflict resolution, look to her and learn.

Take into Account Your Differences

Just because people come from the same family doesn't mean they will have the same values, needs, personalities, and motivations when dealing with each other. Differences generate tension. For example, you may be quiet and reserved while your mom is gregarious and outspoken. This personality difference can be a source of conflict.

You and your mom will have different needs at various times in your relationship. And you may be motivated by different people, events, and beliefs. It is also possible to adopt different values as an adult: for example, a daughter who was raised as a Catholic becomes Protestant; a daughter raised with no spiritual beliefs becomes a believer in Christ. These differences can lead to moments of friction.

Strategies for Handling Conflict

Whether you have different needs, motivations, values, beliefs, ways of doing things, personalities, or traits, learning to handle those differences well will improve your mother-daughter relationship. In this section, I'll outline strategies that can help.

Use the Problem-Solving Approach

When you and your mother have a conflict, follow these steps to reconciliation. They are similar to the problem-solving model presented in chapter 1:

Identify the conflict. Rather than fighting or internalizing the problem or making accusations that she is uncaring, unfair, or whatever, tell your mom you are having a conflict or disagreement. For example, you might say, "Mom, I'm having a problem with how much time you spend with my sister." Recognize it as your problem involving her.

Bring up the conflict in order to solve the problem. Don't sit on it and allow tension to build. And don't go on the attack. Decide to calmly bring up the issue at a time conducive to talking and action. In other words, don't mention the problem as you walk out the door, or when your mom is upset by another phone call, or when you are tired and irritable. Pick a good time and place to raise the issue.

Agree on what the problem actually is. Some problems never get resolved because there is a lack of agreement about the nature of the problem. To clarify, both of you say what the problem is and make sure you agree that you are talking about the same issue. Using the example above, your mom might feel that the problem is that you are too sensitive to the time she spends with your sister, that you are making an issue where there is none. In this case, you don't have agreement on the problem. She feels the problem is your sensitivity. You feel she is being partial. Two different issues are at work. Get agreement first.

Let each person give her view of the problem. Each of you say what and why you think the problem exists. Listen to each other and understand each other's perspective. Then define the problem, as we discussed in chapter 1.

Measure the problem. How long has the problem existed, how often does it happen, and when it happens, how long does it go on? Typically nothing happens "always" and "never," yet we frequently use these words. Be realistic. If you aren't sure, track the problem and see how often or how long it happens. Even if something happens only once, it can be a big deal. For example, if your mother betrayed a secret with which you entrusted her, a one-time betrayal is still serious. In general, however, the more frequent or chronic a problem, the more difficult change becomes.

Make suggestions as to how to resolve the issue. Solutions are needed. Each of you propose a few. Whatever you think may help remedy the situation, suggest it.

Come to an agreement as to what to do. Agree on a solution, try it out, and evaluate it over time. Come back in a day, a week, or a month—whatever seems reasonable—and discuss if the new solution is working. At this point, you may have to make modifications or try something else.

Be willing to examine your part in the conflict. So many conflicts are left unresolved because people refuse to acknowledge their part of the problem. They'd rather point the finger. You have to be honest about what your part is and be willing to change or compromise at times.

Learn to Accommodate Style Differences

Identify your conflict style and then your mother's. If you both have similar ways of dealing with conflict, then style is not the issue. On the other hand, it can still cause problems. If you both are fighters, for instance, your conflict styles are compatible, but one or both of you may decide you don't like this style. It may not be kind or biblically recommended. Fighters don't always resolve conflict. In those cases, review the problem-solving strategy outlined above.

Or you both may have compatible styles of conflict avoidance. Again, the problem isn't that the styles clash, but that important issues never get raised and resolved. Avoiders have to muster the courage to bring up relationship problems. Again, review the problem-solving model for guidance.

If the problem is that your styles of dealing with conflict are incompatible, you may have to learn to accommodate your mom's style or modify yours. Here are some tips as to how to do this:

One of you is an avoider, and the other is a fighter. The avoider needs to push herself to bring up problems. If you're the avoider, use your voice and don't be afraid of what this will do to the relationship. The fighter needs to practice the cool-down strategies described in chapter 2. Take a deep breath, count to ten or take a ten-minute time-out, be slow to speak and quick to listen. Don't yell, blame, name-call, or bring up the past. Stick to the issue at hand. Pray for more self-control. Follow fair-fighting rules such as:

- The disagreement should be based on some reality rather than emotion.
- Control your tongue and your mouth; that is, think before you speak.
- Both of you should participate. Don't let one person do all the talking.
- Desire to come to a resolution.
- Try using humor to minimize the tension.
- Don't bring up the past.
- Focus on the problem, not the person.

One of you is calm and rational, and the other is a fighter. Sometimes people who are fighters think those who aren't don't care.

Calm and rational responses to conflict can be mistaken for a lack of passion. This isn't necessarily true. If your mom is calm and you want to fight, avoid trying to bait her into an argument. This usually happens when you blame, name-call, or bring up issues from the past. If your mom is a fighter and you are the calm one, stay calm and ask her to take a deep breath, slow down, and take a time-out if necessary. Explain to her that you have trouble listening or understanding what she needs when she is yelling.

One is calm, and the other is an avoider. The one who avoids conflict needs to be encouraged to bring up problems and reassured that this will actually strengthen intimacy. It's hard to be intimate with someone when you tiptoe around conflict. Dealing with conflict feels uncomfortable to avoiders, but that isn't a reason to continue to avoid it. Like most things, your discomfort will lessen as you practice new behaviors. If your mother is the avoider, encourage her to share what she thinks or feels, then move through the problem-solving process. The message needs to be that this relationship is a safe place to practice confronting difficult issues. As you and your mom are able to share more of your intimate thoughts and feelings, you will grow closer.

One of you accommodates but then feels resentful. If one of you accommodates just to avoid the discomfort of conflict, don't! This style of dealing with conflict often leads to hidden anger and resentment. Over time, this isn't a good strategy. Occasional accommodation or accommodation that is not resented is fine and even helpful when solving problems. But when accommodation becomes a source of resentment, try being more assertive. Find your voice and use it, following the problem-solving model described previously. Don't give in unless you really feel OK about relinquishing your position or changing your mind.

Follow a Biblical Model of Settling Conflict

Because conflict is a part of our human relationships, Jesus gave instructions as to how to handle and settle disputes. His instructions are recorded in Matthew 18, a chapter often cited for procedural rules. There are also several other scriptures that give wisdom regarding the handling of conflicts. No matter what your conflict-handling style is, biblical instruction calls all of us into account. We do well to follow these guidelines.

Face the conflict (see Matthew 18:15). Jesus tells us to go to the person who has wronged, offended, or sinned against us. We are to acknowledge the problem and the impact it has on our relationship. Go immediately and directly to the person involved and discuss the problem.

Bring in a mediator if necessary (see Matthew 18:16–17). If the person involved won't listen or work to resolve the problem one-on-one, we are instructed to bring mediators or witnesses to help work things out. This is why mothers and daughters come to counseling; they want someone to mediate the conflict and help them resolve the problem. You can go to another family member, a friend, a minister, priest, rabbi, etc. An objective party can help. Be careful not to pull in a family member just to side with you. Rather, find someone who will not take sides but help you mediate the problem.

Forgive (see Philippians 4:4–7). Once you have resolved the conflict, you are to forgive the person and live in harmony, rejoicing in the Lord. Forgiveness will be discussed in more detail in chapter 9.

Move beyond the conflict. The apostle Paul reminds us to not only forgive those with whom we have had conflict but to move beyond that conflict and not hold a grudge. Jesus desires that we live in peace with each other. This is only possible as we follow His greatest commandment: to love the Lord with all our heart and our neighbor as we love ourselves (Matthew 22:37–40).

The gospel emphasizes the redemption of humankind made possible through the sacrifice of Christ. Because of that redemption, Christians are to resolve conflict in the spirit of love and reconciliation. Punishment and judgment are left to God's mercy and grace. This means we should do whatever possible to live in harmony with each other. Resolve your mother-daughter disputes. Love your mother with the love of Christ. Be reconciled to her, tenderhearted; forgive her because Christ forgave you.

Here are a few scriptures that make these points:

- God calls us to live in peace (see 1 Corinthians 7:15).
- Love endures all things (see 1 Corinthians 13:7).
- Remove the plank in your eye before you try to get rid of the plank in hers (see Matthew 7:3–5).
- Use mercy to relieve tension and have a more patient and tolerant spirit (see Micah 6:8).
- If you can't settle a disagreement before "the sun goes down" (see Ephesians 4:26), at least begin the process.

Establish Boundaries

One of the important tasks for adult daughters and mothers to do is to set boundaries for their relationship. If you haven't done this and boundaries are a problem, it's time to have a talk. Better to discuss the parameters of your relationship *before* trouble emerges rather than *during* a conflict.

One reason boundaries are so important is because mothers and daughters often have different expectations about their relationship. Both also come from different generations involving different life tasks. According to Karen Fingerman's study, it appears that mothers tend to have more invested in their relationship with their adult daughter and have more time to give to her. The daughter, on the other hand, feels more intruded upon, criticized, and unable to give the time and attention she perceives is needed.[3] These findings suggest that mothers may want more time and attention than their adult daughters can and will give. Therefore, boundaries need to be negotiated and set.

If boundaries are a problem, set aside a time to have a discussion with your mom. Simply say, "Mom, let's talk about what you expect from me and what I expect from you, given our lives and all that is in them. Here's what I'm thinking . . .What are you thinking?"

If you have a specific issue you want to address, use the problem-solving model to tackle it. For example, one common problem I hear about is mothers who drop in unexpectedly and disrupt the daughter's day or plans. If that is your issue, work through all the steps until you've resolved the problem. The goal is to come to an agreement about what is expected and then try to honor those boundaries with each other.

If you come to an agreement and Mom breaks that agreement, remind her to respect what you have established. New behavior doesn't happen overnight. Be patient. Instead of becoming angry or critical, say something like, "Mom, remember, you weren't going to do this. We agreed." Then see if she does better the next time. Praise her efforts and her willingness to change. Help each other remember the importance of being respectful to the other's wishes.

Try Ignoring

Some irritating behaviors or personality traits can simply be ignored. For example, one adult daughter I know is bothered by her mother and father's bad table manners. After years of talking about the problem with no change, she decided to ignore the problem and not get all worked up over it. Meals and visits go better. This is hardly an issue she wants to fight about every visit.

Some people find it more difficult to ignore such situations. If you tend to avoid conflict, you are probably better at ignoring than people who want to reduce every relationship tension. Ignoring a problem is different than avoiding it. When you ignore, you choose not to make the problem an issue because it really isn't a big issue causing relationship problems. Avoiding a problem means you aren't dealing with an issue that is significant, and this is causing relationship problems. If you are a fighter, you may want to consider this strategy and not make a mountain out of every mole hill. Parents use ignoring strategies with teens all the time. If a parent jumped on her teen for every small annoyance, there would be no positive moments in the relationship! Although I'm exaggerating, you get the point. Sometimes we do best to ignore irritating habits when it comes to our mom. After all, our life goal isn't to fix her and make her acceptable to our way of thinking and living!

When you use ignoring to handle conflict, it helps to physically look and move away from the person and not say anything. Then make eye contact again when the behavior stops. In the example above, the daughter didn't look at her mom when she chewed with her mouth open. It was easier to ignore the bad table manners when she didn't "see" them. She had a more pleasant meal experience, and her mother didn't feel her daughter was looking down at her.

Now, of course you don't use ignoring for serious behavior problems such as drinking, depression, or abuse. In those cases, you need to set boundaries and possibly work with a therapist. I'm only talking about ignoring those little quirks our parents have that are harmless but irritating.

Check Your Thoughts and Beliefs

Our thoughts and beliefs can bring on conflict. For example, if you tell me, "My mom isn't sensitive to my time," this statement is based on a belief you hold. In your mind, it matters why that statement seems true. Here are some possible reasons why you may believe this:

"She is a horrible manager of time herself."

"She is too busy to notice how busy I am."

"My mom has never been sensitive to me."

"My mom is on a different time schedule now that she is retired, and she forgets how busy a day gets with children."

Each of these reasons takes you down a different path. One may lead you to feel angry or hurt. Others are more empathetic. Still others allow for understanding of your mom's differences.

Whatever you believe to be true influences how you will respond and whether or not that thought will create conflict. Typically, the more hurt and wounded you are from the past and the more uncertain you are about yourself, the more likely you are to get into conflicts whether or not you acknowledge them. Why? Because there is a good chance you will attribute a negative thought to the conflict.

That was the case with Rachel and her mom. For years, Rachel's mother was depressed and functioned poorly in how she cared for Rachel as a child. Rachel remembers her mother in bed most of the time she lived at home. Mom was viewed as fragile and unable to cope with life. Consequently Rachel learned not to depend on her for anything she needed and became rather self-sufficient.

When Rachel was thirty-two, her mom received treatment for depression and dramatically improved. She then offered to baby-sit Rachel's young son. Now that Mom's mood was improved, she functioned so much better and participated more fully in life. But Mom's desire to baby-sit became a source of conflict between mother and daughter. Rachel was reluctant to let her mom baby-sit her son based on past memories of her mom's depression and inability to function.

Rachel's thoughts were: *How can I trust her to be better? I know this is crazy, but a part of me even resents her taking care of my son and not taking care of me. I feel angry, and yet this is a good thing my mom wants to do. I guess it's resentment I feel. I don't want her to baby-sit. I'm too angry about the past.*

What, on the surface, looked like a nice gesture from a mother to a daughter was really a loaded issue from the past that led to conflict. It happened because there was unresolved baggage from the past affecting the way Rachel thought about her mom. Before Rachel was ready to allow her mom to baby-sit, she had to deal with her hurt and anger; she had to forgive her mom and reconcile with her.

Your thoughts are influenced by your beliefs, and they lead you to feel certain ways. If your thoughts about your mom are mostly negative, examine your beliefs. Do you believe your mother doesn't love you, wants to hurt you, or doesn't care about you? If so, you may need counseling to work through these difficult perceptions.

Generally, mothers love and care about their daughters and want the best for them. They may have trouble showing love in healthy ways, and they may be uninformed or inconsistent because of their own problems. But usually love is an underlying motive.

If you can embrace a more positive view of your mom in general, your thoughts may be less negative. Give her the benefit of the doubt until she proves you wrong. Ask about her motivations. Listen to what she says, and don't be so quick to attribute your thinking to her. Her thoughts may be different.

In my relationship with my mom, I have found that my own negative thoughts about her behavior are often predicated on my thinking, which is influenced by all kinds of things. When she explains why she does what she does, I don't always agree with her, but

I know her behavior is motivated out of love and care. I genuinely believe my mother loves and cares about her children and would sacrifice the world for them.

Until I had this understanding, my perceptions caused problems. Here's an example of something that caused conflict for years until I had a discussion with her. I always felt unattractive, growing up with red hair and very white skin while living in a beach town. The popular girls were the blonde, blue-eyed wealthy ones who lived on the beach and had suntans. When I entered junior high and my body was changing, I, like all the other girls, felt awkward about my looks and the changes occurring in my body. At that time in my life, my mother wanted to reinforce my academic potential. She had a frank conversation with me, saying (in my mind) that I didn't have great looks but I was smart and had a good personality. I was devastated! This only reinforced my feelings of unattractiveness. In my mind, even my own mother confirmed my fear! I was unattractive!

This bothered me for years—so much so that I always made sure I had attractive boyfriends and that I worked on my personality and grades. As an adult (and as a therapist), I was able to talk about this with my mom. I asked if she remembered this conversation, and she didn't. But she did tell me she was concerned that I use all the gifts God gave me and didn't become some airheaded woman who focused only on looks and not on other important attributes. She wanted to raise an independent and strong daughter (like herself). She did, and for that I am so grateful.

But somewhere along the way, I attributed her concern negatively. Because we didn't discuss it (I never brought it up, and she didn't know what I felt), it created conflict. Once I raised the issue, asked her to explain, and learned her true heart and concern for me, it was no longer an issue between us. How easily daughters can perceive the wrong intention or motive from our mom! Often it is because we are hurt or upset by something or someone else. Our perceptions can distort the actions and thoughts of others.

How often do you get upset with your mom? Are there occasional upsets or ongoing irritations? Whatever the case, begin to address those areas of hurt and wounding. I realize that in some cases, mothers can be the source of the hurt. Confronting the hurt may not lead to any change or even an acknowledging of a problem. If you've been hurt by the words or action of your mother and there seems to be no way to resolve it, forgive her and move on with your life. Of course, this sounds like it should be easy to do. It may not be. In fact, because it can be so difficult, I've devoted a whole chapter to that topic (see chapter 9).

Some disagreements will have to remain disagreements because conflict resolution requires the participation of two people. Forgiveness is a personal act. Reconciliation may not be possible, only forgiveness. If your mother is unwilling to sit at the table of resolution, then accept this as a relationship loss. Grieve and let go of the wish for a better mom.

If your mother is no longer alive, you will not be able to reconcile old hurts, but you can forgive and try to understand why she did what she did. Sometimes that understanding brings empathy, tolerance, and relief.

When possible, do whatever you can to make peace with your mother. Your efforts will be rewarded. Reconciliation is a useful life skill; practice conflict resolution with those who are willing to participate. As you become more confident, try to reconcile a small issue before you move on to bigger ones. With practice, love, understanding, patience, kindness, gentleness, and time, you can work out your differences. Be a peacemaker who doesn't avoid conflict but dives in to resolve it.

These opening chapters have offered specific strategies for

improving your relationship with your mother so that you can work through problems and develop a rewarding relationship. In the next chapters I'll broaden our focus a bit and help you see the foundation for many of the conflicts that affect the mother-daughter relationship. My goal is not only to help you understand your relationship with your mother but also to give you perspectives on making the relationship with your daughter the best it can be.

THOUGHT POINTS

1. Do you think conflict with your mom is a "normal" part of your relationship? Is there conflict in your relationship that needs to be resolved? If so, identify the issues causing the anger.

2. Using the fifteen questions on pages 76–77 concerning how you deal with conflict, identify your and your mother's basic conflict style (calm and rational, fighter, avoider, accommodator, compromiser). Are your two styles different? If so, how will you help to make changes to accommodate your mother's style?

3. Consider the differences you and your mom have that play into your conflicts. Examples might be personality, life stage, values, beliefs, and needs.

4. Review the problem-solving approach and biblical guidelines starting on pages 83 and 87. Are you working through these steps?

5. Are boundaries a problem for you? If so, discuss in what ways they are causing difficulties in your relationship with your mom.

6. How much do you think negative thinking and beliefs get in the way of resolving problems between you and your mom? What negative thoughts do you have that may be causing problems?

7. Is ignoring a strategy that would help you handle some annoyances? If so, which ones?

8. Are you willing to work on reconciliation with your mom? If the answer is no, then choose to forgive.

5

GREAT EXPECTATIONS: LIVING OUR MOTHER'S DREAMS

ONCE UPON A TIME a beautiful daughter was born to a physician and his wife in the kingdom of Is. Everyone swooned and crooned at the beauty of this baby. "She will do her parents proud. This child will accomplish great things," they said.

Her mother smiled and thought, *You will do all the things I was afraid to do. I was a nurse; you'll be a doctor. I am shy; you'll be outgoing. I get anxious; you'll be confident. I retreat under pressure; you'll move forward. In you, all my hopes and dreams will come true. You will be what I never thought it possible to be.*

As the daughter grew, problems came to the kingdom. The daughter was not outgoing and confident, and she didn't want to be a doctor. She fainted at the sight of blood. "I want to be a famous dancer," the child declared.

"No, no, you mustn't!" her mother insisted. "You are destined to become a great physician. No more dancing. You must study your Latin and Greek. Listen to me, and do as I say."

"But I have no interest in these things," the daughter loudly proclaimed.

A Daughter's Journey Home

"Your interests don't matter," her mother said. "Your life has been planned. A physician you will become. Now study your Latin."

The dutiful daughter obeyed, although her heart wasn't in it. Her mind wandered, and she dreamed of the ballet, of costumes and music, and . . . She must stop dreaming, she told herself, because her dreams were only that: foolish dreams. Saddened, the daughter began to write. Her love for the ballet came out in wonderful stories in which, adorned in beautiful costumes, she danced before kings and moved with great ease, free to express herself. Others noticed her grace and applauded her creativity and talent. But then her thoughts returned to the reality of her life. Her writing changed:

I danced in my room.
Look, Mommy, see what I can do. I can go up on my toes and make a turn.
But my mother turned her eyes and said,
"Stop that or you'll get hurt."

I danced at my school.
Please come and see, Mommy.
I am a beautiful swan who glides across the stage.
But my mother was too busy to come.
"Such nonsense. I don't have time for such nonsense."

Then I danced at the theatre.
Surely you will come and see me as the prima ballerina.
I have the most important part.
But my mother never came.
"Foolish girl. You need a job, a real job."
For when I danced, I was living my dreams
and not my mother's.

With tears dropping on the paper, the daughter threw the poem in the trash. As she slept that night, her mother found the crumbled paper and slowly smoothed out the wrinkles. What private thoughts did her daughter harbor? Carefully, she read the poem and began to weep. Why had she not seen this? By living the mother's dreams, her daughter was dying to her own. Blinded by ambition and good intentions, the mother never realized her expectations were killing her daughter's gentle spirit. She would make things right.

Gently she awakened the sleeping daughter and whispered in her ear. "Tomorrow you shall dance."

The daughter smiled and rolled back to sleep. It was a wonderful dream. *If only dreams could come true,* she thought.

From the moment we are conceived, expectations begin to form. First there is the hope of a healthy daughter: Count the toes and fingers. Everything's in the right place, isn't it? Whew! What a relief. Then comes the familial examination: "She has your ears, the shape of my toes, . . . Oh no! . . . The nose . . . Let's hope she gets yours and breaks the curse!"

There is something magical about this combination of genetic codes. We look on in awe, and as our daughters grow and their personalities emerge, we are quick to assign praise or blame: "She's got your family's stubbornness." Or, "How about that temper? Reminds me of your mother." Or, "She's so patient. I know that comes from my family."

There are the comparisons, the differences, but mostly there are expectations—the great expectations mothers have that their little daughters will grow up to become role models, leaders, women of faith, super moms, teachers, doctors . . . extraordinary women. Mothers pray they won't make the same mistakes their own mothers did; they want their daughters to learn from their examples and not be burdened by the same worries they carried themselves for too many years. Mothers hope their daughters will be freer, more self-assured, more focused and courageous.

These are the generalized hopes and expectations most mothers have for their daughters. The problems arise when a mother has specific dreams for her daughter that differ from those the daughter has for herself, illustrated by the mother in the story who wanted her dance-loving daughter to become a physician. In this chapter, I'd like you to examine the expectations within your mother-daughter relationship: the expectations you felt your mother had for you, the expectations you may be putting on your own daughter—and also, a little later, the expectations you hold for your mother.

Usually, mothers do not intend to squelch their daughters' dreams. But it happens. Sometimes mothers are simply unaware of what their daughters truly desire, or they're afraid for them to explore new things, or they want to live vicariously through their daughters' experiences. Other times, mothers are too tied up with their own emotional needs to consider those of another, or they are so fearful that they dare not dream themselves and thus can't imagine their daughters having dreams either.

THE TWO SIDES OF EXPECTATIONS

Daughters often feel pressured to live up to the dreams and hopes of both parents. This can be a good thing when realistic expectations coincide with the daughter's aspirations and challenge her. Expectations can help her grow as a person.

For example, I knew my daughter, Katie, could handle a more challenging piano piece. Her teacher concurred and assigned her a new classical number. Katie balked when she first saw the piece, insisting that it was too hard and that she would never learn it. Both the teacher and I knew this wasn't true. She just needed to be challenged to a new level of performance. Katie worked hard on the piece and performed it beautifully. Even she was surprised and pleased at how well she did. In this case, my expectation was realistic and challenged Katie to new heights.

Other times, however, expectations cause unnecessary anxiety and pressure. One young woman I treated slept only two to three hours a night because she spent so much time studying. She couldn't risk being anything less than the best and was obsessed with getting perfect grades. Part of her healing was having her parents give her permission to get a B—or even to fail. We even assigned her to fail at something. Her push to be perfect was an unrealistic expectation causing her great anxiety and distress.

As daughters reach adolescence and become more independent from their mom, some discover that their innate push for autonomy is not always welcomed and may be met with resistance from their mother. Some daughters may act out or become disobedient in order to test their emerging confidence and autonomy. As they look to Mom to confirm their sense of self and their growing independence, they expect to be reinforced in their efforts. This is a realistic expectation daughters have of their mother. When moms (and dads) don't give this confirmation, daughters may try to please Mom by living out the mother's dreams and expectations for the daughter in order to receive Mom's approval. However, in the long run, this backfires on both of them by creating resentment and restlessness.

Moms have to be so careful not to force their dreams on their daughters! It can happen in small, subtle ways, so mothers have to be vigilant. I could give you multiple examples of how often I catch myself doing this. There is such a fine line between motivating my daughter to try new things and pushing my dreams to be hers.

A few years ago, my daughter was competing in a speech tournament. I was coaching her as to how she should present her poem. The more persistent and explicit I became, the more frustrated she became.

At one point, she looked me straight in the eye and said, "That's how you would do it, but I would do it differently."

She was right. I backed down and apologized. "Tell me how you would interpret this poem. I'm listening," I told her.

Another time she caught me again. I love the cello and always wished I had learned to play it. My hope was that one of my children would choose the cello so I could enjoy its music through them. Well, I suggested, then I pushed, then I kept suggesting—even though both children had already chosen another instrument. Finally my very astute daughter had had enough; she said, "Mom, you wanted to play the cello. We don't."

I got the message loud and clear: Stop pushing your agenda on us.

It's easy for us moms to push our dreams onto our children. But we must let go of the expectation that our daughters will become who we think they should be. Instead, we need to help them be who they uniquely are and accept them without condition, not mold them into clones of ourselves.

Listen and Ask Questions

To guide our daughters in becoming the women God intends them to be, we mothers have to listen more and ask questions. First ask *yourself* questions: What excites my daughter? What does she feel passionate about? What would she like to try? What is she afraid of? What about that situation bothers her?

The answers to questions like these reveal your daughter's desires and heart. They also help you sort out which dreams are your own and which ones are your daughter's. For example, when my daughter had to give an oral presentation in front of her class the first time, she hesitated because she was worried she would make a mistake. Her fear was that someone would laugh at her. I told her that yes, that could happen. She might make a mistake, and someone might laugh. But I also talked about the importance of not giving other people the power to stop you from trying.

Then I shared a story about how I had messed up, laughed at myself, and tried again. I couldn't control how other people reacted to my mistake, but I could control the way I reacted. I certainly didn't want those people to stop me from trying again! By sharing the story of a time when I was scared and, sure enough, I failed, I gave her permission to make a mistake too. The lesson was important because she saw me as always confident and unafraid to speak. She needed to know I didn't start out that way.

EXPECTATIONS AND BODY IMAGE

Mothers and daughters also need to think about the expectations they have about their physical body. A family's, and especially a mother's, expectations can lead a daughter to believe she must be perfect in all that she does—and is. These daughters are highly anxious, constantly worried that they may fail and that they can never measure up to the self-imposed or family-imposed standards of perfection. Often we see these girls in therapy for help in dealing with an eating disorder.

The comments and attitudes mothers verbalize about their own body image are also translated to their daughters. Do you degrade yourself and constantly complain about your physical imperfections? If you do, notice how self-degradation influences your daughter. Soon you'll probably hear her complaining that her thighs are too big or her breasts are too small. And let's face it; she doesn't need her mother's angst added to all the cultural obsession with beauty that she'll encounter.

I'll never forget the time I stepped out of the shower when Katie was still very young. She eyed me up and down and sized up her mom's mature female body. Then she asked, "Mom, will I get that crinkly stuff on your legs? It doesn't look too good."

I laughed. She was looking at the cellulite on my thighs. "Well," I responded, "you might, but if you do, it's no big deal. Not too many of us have the perfect legs we see in magazines or on TV. And when I was younger, I didn't have this crinkly stuff. This is how most women my age look—and it's fine."

Honestly, I tried my best to be convincing. The truth is, I've always disliked the cellulite on my thighs, but I've come to terms with it. It doesn't define me or shake my confidence, and I wanted her to hear that. In today's world, daughters need mothers who are not obsessed with body image in order to help them accept their own bodies. They need women with realistic physical expectations whose sense of self is not defined solely by outward appearance.

Creating an Atmosphere for Dialogue

If you're the mother of a daughter, you have to work at creating an atmosphere in which you and your daughter can share feelings without feeling judged. Help your daughter feel safe when she wants to talk to you. By your example, help her understand how she can create that safe place to allow you to express your thoughts to her— and someday, for her daughter to do the same! Once you both feel safe in sharing your thoughts, you can problem-solve ways to handle difficult situations and to pursue goals. Mothers need to take the lead and create an atmosphere of open communication.

Ginger's mom was able to create that safe place for her daughter when her daughter became pregnant by a married man. Although heartbroken for her daughter, Ginger's mom was determined to help her problem-solve what to do.

At first Ginger was afraid to talk to her mom, fearing her judgment and knowing she had greatly disappointed her mother. But Mom began the dialogue. "Ginger, I would be lying if I told you I wasn't disappointed. I am," she said. "But I still love you and want to hear what you are thinking and feeling about all of this."

Ginger opened up. She was having trouble forgiving herself and working through her anger. How could she be so foolish to have thought this man would leave his wife for her? There were never any signs of this.

The two women prayed together, and Ginger confessed her failures. Her mom reminded her that everyone makes mistakes but that we serve a God of grace. She had asked Him to forgive her, and He had. Now it was time to stop beating herself up and make a plan. Ginger decided to have the baby and place him or her for adoption. The father agreed to the decision as well.

Both Ginger and her mom attended a group to work through the loss associated with Ginger's situation. Out of all that happened, Ginger said, "My mom was incredible. What I expected her to do, she didn't. I expected her to yell at me, tell me I was loser, and have nothing to do with me. She didn't. Instead she was real and admitted being disappointed, sometimes angry, and sometimes depressed. She had a lot of feelings that were hard for me to see, but she was helpful when I turned to her for help. After this, I feel I could go to her for anything."

HANDLING MOM'S UNREALISTIC EXPECTATIONS

But what happens if you're the daughter, and your mom doesn't have realistic expectations and isn't reasonable, as Ginger's mom was? What if there's a situation now when you, as an adult, find yourself in a difficult spot and your mother doesn't listen and is judgmental and critical?

In those cases, you need to be assertive. Not *aggressive* but *assertive*. Being aggressive means you attack argumentatively, you bully, and maybe you even threaten those with whom you disagree. Assertiveness means you don't give in to the wants of others when you disagree with them, but you also don't keep silent and expect people to read your mind. Assertiveness means not yelling at people and demanding your way but speaking up for what you need or want. It is a useful skill for all relationships.

There are two parts to being assertive: First, know what you want, and second, say it. One of the reasons many of us don't practice being assertive is because we don't know what we want! Too often we are wishy-washy, unsure, and undefined. Or we feel guilty and don't believe we have the right to speak up. As a result we allow others to manipulate us into doing things we don't want to do or don't have time to do and then feel resentful when we're overloaded with unpleasant responsibilities.

As an adult, you don't have to sit by and remain helplessly silent. Your relationship with your mom will improve if you learn to speak up assertively—in a way that is not rude or provoking but in a manner that lets your feelings be heard. Be assertive about your mother's expectations that are unrealistic.

Of course, you first have to know what you want and need. Many adult daughters have complaints but don't know what would be better; they haven't thought through the situation. Well, think about it! What would help take the pressure off the unrealistic expectations that are operating in your relationship with your mom?

Here's how to work through a mother-daughter problem and be assertive in the way you present your needs:

Evaluate the situation. Do you feel that what is being asked of you is realistic? Are you bothered by your mom's expectations? If you don't act, will you feel resentful, upset, anxious, or "down"? Decide if this is the time to speak up.

Consider the timing. Decide *when* you need to address the issue. Should you speak up immediately, or do you need time to think about how you feel and how best to present those feelings? Consider the consequences of addressing the situation. Perhaps you want to organize your thoughts to make sure you're reacting to the right issue, or maybe you need time to build your courage. Knowing when to confront is important. For example, it may be better to bring up your mother's unrealistic expectations when the two of you are alone, rather than when the extended family has gathered for a holiday meal. Time your assertiveness for a moment that is conducive to listening and responsiveness.

Identify the problem. Be specific. Don't expect your mother to read your mind or magically guess what is distressing you. Say exactly what the problem is and how it is affecting you. Address a specific expectation.

Say how you feel. No one *causes* you to feel things. You allow yourself to feel certain ways. Don't blame others. For example, instead of saying, "You make me feel inadequate when you criticize my parenting," say, "I feel inadequate when you criticize my parenting." Your intent is to communicate your feeling (from your point of view) that is associated with her behavior.

Say what you want to have happen. This is the tough but important part. You need to know what you want and what would help the situation. For example, you might say, "Mom, I can't be available every moment you need me. I would love to say I could, but that's not realistic. I know it's been tough for you since Dad died. I'll do what I can when I can, but there are limits to the amount of help I can give."

It is important to communicate a solution or a desire so that your mom has a clear idea of the problem and the limits of what you are willing and able to do to help with it. This doesn't guarantee she'll accept what you're saying, but at least you've communicated your position and can negotiate from there.

107

Sarah had to practice being more assertive with her mother. In the past, she had withdrawn when her mom became critical. She decided she needed to address her mom's unrealistic expectations of her. Here's an example of what she did. Sarah's mother is a great cook, and she expected her daughters to share her love of and talent for preparing elaborate, gourmet meals. One daughter shared the mother's skills and enthusiasm for the culinary arts. But Sarah didn't. Every time her mother came to visit, she made a negative comment about Sarah's bad cooking. Sarah admits she's not a great cook, but her meals were nutritional and adequate. And no one in Sarah's family complained.

Sarah decided to say something to her mom. She evaluated the situation, thought through what she would say, and found a time when they were alone. "Mom, I am very hurt by your comments regarding my cooking," she said. "I know I'm not a fabulous cook like you or my sister, but my family is satisfied with my meals, and so am I. I feel bad when you say what you do, and I don't enjoy our visits. I won't ever be the cook you would like me to be. For one thing, I have no interest in cooking. So, Mom, I would like you to stop making the negative comments."

Sarah's mom was a little miffed at first, but she backed off her comments about Sarah's cooking. Sarah noticed her mom's efforts and thanked her for making the change. As a result, both mother and daughter looked forward to visiting each other.

Our Unrealistic Expectations of Mom

When I was writing this book, women often asked me what subject I was writing about. When I told them it was about mothers and daughters, immediately they reacted with, "Oh, you should interview me. Let me tell you about my mom." This reaction was almost universal. Obviously, mothers make a lasting impression on their daughters. And apparently, we all have complaints about them. It seems to be normal!

But it's not only mothers who have unrealistic expectations for their daughters, however. Daughters, too, have great expectations for their mother. In therapy, I've seen many adult daughters who won't give up expecting their mom to be someone she isn't and never will be. They can't accept reality and are constantly trying to change their mother or hoping someday to win that unconditional love or acceptance they never had as a child. So they hold on to an idealized picture of Mom and put their lives on hold until she magically becomes that picture.

There is always hope that maturity will bring a new appreciation on both sides of mother-and-daughter struggles. And sometimes it happens; these daughters with unrealistic expectations of their mother finally "grow up" and abandon their dreams of having an all-loving, all-powerful, all-accepting mom. Confirming this tendency, researcher Karen Fingerman found that the bond between mother and daughter shifts as both age. Generally, it moves from an idealized interconnectedness in young adulthood to a sophisticated inter-dependence between the two women later in life.[1] We assume that this "sophisticated" relationship includes each woman's acceptance of the other as she is, not as the other fantasized that she would be.

Do you feel that your mom has let you down? That she hasn't lived up to your expectations of her? When we feel our mom has failed us, we often become disillusioned. But frankly, we expect too much of Mom. After all, mothers are human, too, and struggle with their own baggage from generations of family history. Moms are not God. They are imperfect women.

Most of us understand intellectually that our mom isn't perfect, but that doesn't seem to stop us from wishing she was. So we make our mom responsible for everything from our self-esteem to our choice of mate. We forget that Mom is a woman in context. She can't give us what she doesn't have. And we forget that we have a free will that often operates outside her influence.

Of course, just as mothers can have *reasonable* expectations of their daughters, so can a daughter have reasonable expectations for Mom. For example, it's reasonable for a child to expect Mom to give her a foundation (values and beliefs), a family history, a female role model, and her life experience. The more Mom works on becoming the woman she was intended to be and authentically shares herself with her daughter, the more the daughter gains from her mother's journey. But if Mom struggles with her own issues of feeling unloved, judged, and inadequate, it is difficult for her to show her daughter anything different. She may try with her words, but her actions speak louder. The result can be a damaged relationship that continues on into adulthood. As authors Elizabeth Debold, Marie Wilson, and Idelisse Malave note, "When a little girl realizes that her mother is not so powerful and may not always provide a safe haven, she experiences loss and betrayal."[2] Because of this reality, we must learn to grieve our loss of the perfect mother.

Take a look at your mom through a wider lens and then determine if your expectations for her are realistic. For example, if your mom is a fearful person, is she really the one you can expect to calm you and help you face your adult fears? Or if your mom rarely received any praise from her parents, will it be natural for her to lavish you with praise? Since you're probably doing this evaluating in hindsight—as an adult looking back on the expectations of your mother that you had as a child—perhaps you can now see that your mother's history made these expectations unrealistic. Now it's time to let go of them and to grieve the loss—in particular, the loss of your dream for a perfect mom.

Our culture expects mothers to be superwomen. When they don't measure up to this ridiculous idea, we feel disappointed or cheated. In fact, we often accuse Mother of ruining our life—blaming her, in particular, for our self-esteem problems. Let me assure you, there are many players in the esteem arena, not just mothers. Yes, there are emotionally disturbed mothers who damage their children, but these children often live in and come from emotionally disturbed families or problem-plagued environments that contribute to their problems as well. The bulk of mothers are not disturbed and are not deliberately trying to destroy their daughters.

The problem is that we are looking for esteem from the wrong source. Typically we try to get it from our accomplishments or other people. Then, when we fail at a task or when someone lets us down, we are devastated. We feel we need approval, acceptance, and unconditional love. And while I would agree that all those qualities are necessary for esteem, I would direct you to the only place possible to get it—through an intimacy with God. We have no real esteem apart from Him.

We are esteemed because He chose us and loves us unconditionally. Nothing we do gives us esteem in God's eyes. We have God's esteem because we are His, made in His image and loved. No matter what your mothering experience, you are highly esteemed by God. If you can grasp and believe this, it will help you find esteem even if you came from the most devastating family circumstances.

You see, God didn't leave us to the mercy of family baggage and other people. He sent His Son so we could have the necessary emotional and relational correction we needed regardless of family background or history. Yes, it's important to work on our mother-daughter relationship and confront hurts and criticisms. But if your mother didn't or wasn't able to give you the loving foundation that was expected of her, you are not doomed to poor self-esteem and life-long feelings of inadequacy. You can break free from a negative self-image by looking to God to find your esteem. This may sound like a cliché, but it is true. As you renew your mind and soul with the Word of God, you will see how incredibly loved you are—unconditionally and immeasurably.

Do we all want this kind of love from our mother? Absolutely. But is it realistic to think that our mother can be the correction to all our hurts, wounds, and emotional pain? No.

The only One who can be all-loving, all-knowing. and all-powerful in your life is God. The rest of humanity is flawed and will disappoint. So when your mother doesn't meet your expectation, grieve the loss and turn to God. Find acceptance and love in Him. And keep trying to work it out with your mother.

Daughters Trying to Rescue Mom

In addition to having unrealistic expectations of their mother, many adult daughters try to rescue their mother from her own pain—the pain that may have caused her to be unable to function as capably as was expected of her. If this is your situation, understand that rescuing your mother is not your job. You can feel empathy for your mother's past and the emotional prison it has created for her, but it is not your place to release her. Instead pray that she will have the courage to face her problems and take new action. Point her to those who can support and reinforce her attempts to change. But don't make it your life's goal to be your mom's therapist or to rescue her from her past or current decisions. She, like you, must want to make changes. If she chooses to live in a pained state and deny problems, grieve this as a loss.

Barb realized this fact after years of trying to rescue her mom, Debbie, who had been abused by her father when she was a child. Barb's grandmother—Debbie's mother—never addressed the abuse and stayed with her husband while it continued. When Debbie left home, she married a musician who eventually divorced her, leaving her to rear her two small children on her own. What Debbie didn't know was that, before he left, Barb's father had physically abused Barb.

Barb always felt sorry for her mother because of her past. Divorced, single, and raising two children on a teacher's salary, Debbie's life hadn't been easy. Barb's father made good money but had chosen not to support his family. Now, as an adult, this history weighed heavily on Barb as she wrestled with the effects of her father's abuse. She was becoming increasingly depressed, but she didn't want to burden her mom with her problems; she felt Debbie had enough trouble of her own. Consequently, Barb kept to herself the secret that her father had abused her, and as a result the depression worsened.

Barb felt her mother should have known she was being abused, given Debbie's own history of abuse. When she didn't, Barb felt betrayed. Realizing that she and her mother both needed to bring their situations out into the open in order to get better, Barb tried to talk with her mom about the abuse, but Debbie wouldn't hear of it. It was too painful to recall, and she feared she would fall apart if she began to address it.

Barb offered to get her mom help, but her mother refused. She was clear: the abuse was not something she would address at this time in her life. She believed she would completely fall apart emotionally if she unlocked this painful part of her life. She had to be responsible in her job and couldn't risk an emotional breakdown.

The fact that her mother refused to address the history of abuse led Barb deeper into depression. But, through therapy, Barb came to accept that Debbie's refusal to act was rooted in her fear that she would have a breakdown, lose her job, and have no income to pay bills. Barb didn't like her mother's position, but she realized her mom's avoidance was born out of her family pain, and eventually Barb gave up trying to convince her mom to change her mind. She had thought their shared history of abuse would be an area in which they could also share their pain. She had envisioned herself and her mom working through these issues together—her mom asking forgiveness for not protecting her, and then both being healed and moving forward in their relationship. None of this happened, and Barb had to give up those expectations. But she worked on her own history of abuse with a therapist and learned to grieve her mom's decision as another loss.

Sometimes the ending of the story isn't what we would like. Moms have their own free will and don't always do what we think is right. When this happens, we can stay upset with Mom and say, "Well, she should do this or that," or we can grieve this as a major loss—the loss of a dream—and move on.

Runaway Bunnies

When my daughter was little, together we read the book *The Runaway Bunny* by Margaret Wise Brown.[3] It's a charming story about a little bunny who constantly runs away from his mother. He runs many places, but each time, his mother finds him and reminds him that she will run after him because he is her little bunny.

For a toddler, *The Runaway Bunny* is a wonderful story of reassurance and unconditional love. The message is that no matter where you go or what you do, you can expect your mom will find a way to come after you; she will always be there for you.

But reading this story always left me unsettled, realizing so many of my clients don't have mother bunnies like this. Who really does? Is it realistic to expect mothers to always run after us and find us, no matter what kind of trouble we land in? Is it even wise? The expectation seems enormous, one of God proportion and unrealistic for earthly beings—even moms. Our mother *doesn't* always find us no matter where we go. She doesn't always know where we are, what we are doing, or how to find us. Sometimes Mom lets us run and make our own mistakes. The hope is that when we come back to her, Mom will still love us.

Only God pursues like the Runaway Bunny's mother. All-knowing, all-giving, all-powerful, He pursues us no matter how far away we've run. And when we run and try to hide, He is always there waiting for us to find Him. He hasn't left.

If you are disappointed in your mom because she doesn't pursue you like the Runaway Bunny's mom, don't be disheartened. Look to your heavenly Father, who never stops pursuing and loving you.

The story concludes with the little bunny finally giving in to his mother's pursuit. "I might as well stay where I am and be your little bunny," he concedes. Although I have no idea what the author intended, this is a strong picture of where God wants us—surrendered to His love. Then we can grieve the losses we've experienced from the not-so-perfect mother we've all had. Ideally, we'll recognize that sometimes her failure to run after us helped us grow. Know that the true Mother Bunny is God, always present, always loving, and always accepting of who you are.

As you grow in your relationship with your mother—or with your daughter—evaluate the expectations you may have for each other. So often, another person's expectations set us up to meet and fulfill all the other person's desires and wishes. She hopes the other person will provide what is missing or somehow complete her. These aren't healthy expectations. We do best when we work on completing ourselves through surrender to God, releasing our past hurts to Him, grieving our losses, and looking only to Him to complete us.

Thought Points

1. What dreams do you feel your mom has for you that you've never fulfilled?

2. What expectations do you, as a daughter, have about your mom that may be unrealistic?

3. Are there losses you need to grieve—expectations that you have held for years that you now realize are unrealistic and have caused relationship difficulties? What are they?

4. Think of ways you could help create an atmosphere that would help you and your mom openly talk.

5. How do you both feel about your physical body? Think about the expectations women face to look a certain way. Are those expectations realistic?

6. Do you ever feel like you need to rescue your mom? Think about those situations and consider a better alternative.

Growing Daughters: Making Meaningful Connections

KATIE SAT ON THE EDGE OF HER BED struggling to put on her shoes.

"Can I help you tie your shoes?"

"No, Mommy. I can do it myself."

The many times we had practiced tying and untying her shoes were coming together in an act of independence. Time for me to let go . . . at least for a moment. As Katie slowly worked the laces, I could see her rising confidence and then her dazzling smile. "See, I did it!"

Do you remember speaking or hearing those words, "I can do it myself"? A daughter's quest for independence begins early. When my daughter proudly (and loudly) proclaimed those words, I had to smile, but at the same time, I also felt sad. Her words signaled a change; she needed me less. Still, I knew it was a healthy step and evidence of her continuing development. I was happy she was beginning to tackle life on her own terms. She *could* do it herself.

As we grow, we move from that safe place of oneness with Mother in the womb to becoming our own person. It's a progressive journey filled with obstacles all along the way, and as we keep moving forward we can get stuck. Loss and emotional pain can stall us. We may experience trauma, a loved one's death, abuse, neglect, abandonment . . . a single event or multiple hurts and woundings. Children rarely have control over what happens to them, and so much can happen in families.

But in many ways it's not so much what losses and traumas we encounter as it is how we respond to those events that determines our progress. Childhood wounds can follow us into adulthood if not resolved. Many of us as adult daughters still need help with our reactions to those hurts.

In the beginning of life, our need for Mother is so powerful it doesn't seem to matter what kind of a mother we had or didn't have. We simply need her, and any absence or separation is difficult. As we grow and come to understand that Mom's absence means she is somewhere else and will eventually return, we can tolerate separation for longer periods of time. Eventually, we initiate the pulling away, although always checking to see if Mom is reliably there. At some point, we are off and running, still checking in now and then to make sure we are moving in the right direction.

Our need for Mom never totally disappears. A part of us is always fighting: we desire oneness with her, and we also need separation. Our task, as daughters, is to become individuals while staying connected to Mom.

THE TRUE VERSUS FALSE SELF

To become uniquely ourselves while maintaining a bond with our mother, we must feel safe to express our true self in the mother-daughter relationship. Ideally, our uniqueness will be celebrated and allowed full expression. But obviously this doesn't always happen; many daughters find themselves creating a "false self" in an attempt to please Mom and present to her the person the daughter thinks she is supposed to be rather than the person she really is.

Kelly was one of those girls. She sat motionless. No expression on her face.

I asked, "Kelly, what are you feeling right now?"

"Nothing. I feel nothing most of the time. Just this sense of obligation and pressure. I need to perform. To be perfect. No mistakes. Mistakes are just not tolerated in my family. My father is successful but never talks to me or ever asks how I am. My mother has her own ideas about my life. She has chosen a college for me to attend, and my life has been planned out. I'm going to be a lawyer because that's what my mom wants for me. She feels it's a good occupation that will bring me respect."

"Kelly, you've told me a lot about your parents," I said. "Now tell me how you feel."

"I feel . . . I don't know how I feel. I just feel fat."

Kelly is an example of a daughter developing a false identity. In her search for autonomy, she feels stuck and unable to be who she really is. Consequently, she doesn't know who she is. Instead of expressing her true feelings, she is compliant and goes along with the family plan, secretly stuffing her anger inside. All her life, she has been the good and achieving daughter. But inside, she feels differently. She doesn't want to be a lawyer—the profession her family has chosen for her—and she hates the college her mom picked.

Instead of expressing her desires and exercising her true voice, Kelly has developed an eating disorder called anorexia. It is her solution to feared independence. She's angry but doesn't express it. Her mom doesn't ask about her dreams or aspirations, and Kelly keeps them buried.

Kelly's hidden anger and her lack of autonomy are played out through food. Food, she can control. She decides what goes in her body and what doesn't. Her father is distant, her mother preoccupied with appearances and the family's image. Kelly doesn't know how to be Kelly. She fears there is no "self" to be independent. Instead, the anorexia helps her revert to a childlike appearance, forcing her parents to take care of her and deal with her on her terms.

Daughters Grow in Context

Even when mothers pay attention to the developmental and emotional needs of daughters, daughters can still get lost in their quest for autonomy. Why? Because mothers and daughters don't operate in a vacuum. There are other influences that affect a daughter's development. Most daughters live in families with fathers and siblings. And they live in a culture that pulls daily for their attention and may fight the acceptance they find at home.

I want to say this clearly: while mothers exert a great deal of influence and are extremely important to their daughters' growth and development, they are not the only force with which daughters contend. The impact of fathers, of siblings in the family, of extended family members, and of the culture at large are also significant influences on a woman's development and can't be dismissed or diminished. So while I am focusing my efforts to bring peace and connection to the mother-daughter bond, the family therapist in me wants to constantly remind you, when you're looking at problems that arise as a daughter matures, to avoid blame and to widen your lens.

Due to the way our society idealizes mothers, and due to the unrealistic expectations we place on them, we need to actively resist blaming Mom for all our problems. Kelly, in the above story, had to take responsibility for her actions. She was refusing to eat and gain weight. That was not her mother's fault. In fact, Kelly was responding to the emotional distance she felt from both her mother and her father, as well as the incredible pressure she felt from media to look a certain way and the sexual pressures she felt unprepared to face at school. Kelly listened to many voices around her, unable to find her own.

In recent years I have become even more convinced of the need to view a daughter's development through this wider lens of family, media, and community. In my work with mother-daughter pairs, I have seen "good-enough" mothers (a group we'll study in more detail in chapter 11) desperately fight messages delivered by peers and media; I've also seen moms valiantly trying to rescue their daughters from the cultural battles they face, sometimes successfully, other times not. The voices of the culture are loud, forceful, and "in your face." They definitely influence a daughter's sense of who she is.

Today, mothering is such a difficult job because so many competing voices are shouting to define a daughter's identity. Mothers often feel powerless to override the influence of media and the dysfunctional culture in which we live. Their guards are up, their knees are down. Many mothers' battles are fought in prayer.

I often remind new and younger therapists, "Be kinder and gentler to moms. They want to raise healthy daughters. Don't minimize the absence of dads, the abuse of others, the influence of peers, the messages of media, or the pressures of modern life. Daughters grow in context. Many times, they are bombarded by thoughts and ideas counter to their upbringing. Take it all into account. Don't blame. Look at the bigger picture. Sometimes the mother sitting in your therapy office is the only trusted body on whom a daughter feels safe to take out her frustrations. She is not the enemy."

Early in my career, I remember treating a family case that reinforced this thinking. The adult daughter in her twenties was bulimic, the father was alcoholic, and the mother was severely depressed and suicidal. In working with the daughter's bulimia, I felt the mother was too fragile to confront because of her depression. So I was convinced that if I could get the father to stop drinking, then the daughter would stop vomiting. In the family work, I pushed the father to become abstinent. He agreed to try and eventually he stopped drinking. As I guessed, the daughter temporarily stopped vomiting. But to my complete surprise, the mother became suicidal. What went wrong?

A wiser, more experienced therapist who was one of my early mentors helped me understand. For years, the mother had tried desperately to get her husband to stop drinking. Nothing she said or did seemed to make any difference. Her depression was related to feelings of helplessness. The daughter, identifying with the mother's struggles, also tried to get Dad to stop drinking. She, too, was unsuccessful and found herself bingeing and purging in response to similar feelings of powerlessness and helplessness. When I convinced the dad to try sobriety and was successful, the mother felt even more devastated because I, an outsider to the family, was able to temporarily accomplish what she couldn't. The feeling of failure overwhelmed her. It was too much to bear, and she became suicidal.

My correction to the problem was to empower the mother to find a way to deal directly with her husband's drinking. It was her battle to win, not mine. Even though her previous attempts had failed, there were other solutions. With a little help, she confronted the drinking in terms of the effect it had had on her and their daughter. She felt alone and depressed when her husband drank; her daughter felt frightened. With a little coaching, she was no longer willing to be silent about these feelings.

The mother found the courage to speak what was truly in her heart. Feeling empowered and no longer helpless, she dealt with the impact of the husband's destructive drinking behavior on the family. The drinking would stop permanently, or he would leave. She was no longer willing to live with a drunk who operated in denial. When she took her position—one of self-respect and protection for her daughter—he stopped drinking for good. The daughter gave up her food problems, and the mother was no longer depressed. The mother's strong position gave her daughter new courage. The daughter was now ready to confront her dad on a number of hurts she had experienced from him. In this case, the mother's efforts led the way to family healing.

Remember, we aren't here to blame. But we will talk about the impact of family relationships as they influence a daughter's attempts to emotionally separate from her family. Some mothers, like the mother above, are able to take steps of incredible courage and help their daughters become more autonomous, even when the daughters have been wounded in their early lives. Other mothers remain stuck in repetitive family patterns or choose not to make changes. Pain overwhelms them. In those cases, daughters must go it alone.

Perhaps you and your mother are locked in a situation now where a change is needed, but it seems too difficult to contemplate. Whatever your situation, God promises to be by your side, empowering you. Don't get hung up on who should change first, thinking, *She should change because she is my mom. I'll change when she changes.* Maybe she isn't in a position to go first right now, or maybe she just refuses to move at all. No matter, you can move out of that place of helplessness and powerlessness. You can react differently. That is a central message of this book.

Overcoming Dysfunctional Influences

If early experiences and support and reinforcement from family, friends, and the larger community are so important to healthy development, what happens when those elements are withheld or missing? What about those daughters who were not loved or valued early on?

The power of the gospel promises to transform any daughter's life, no matter what her early or family experiences were. This is a truly remarkable and empowering promise, one that can help daughters overcome the effects of families that are woven into destructive patterns of dysfunction. Terry was one of those daughters.

I first met Terry as a depressed teenager. Her life was a mess. Her father had abandoned the family when she was a toddler. Her mother, married and divorced several times, had a new boyfriend. Terry hated her mom's drinking and partying. She repeatedly declined her mother's invitations to party with her; instead, Terry was just trying to concentrate on high school. Tired of her mom's emotional unavailability, she made a point of avoiding her mother as much as possible. Terry just wanted to graduate and leave home.

One night Terry attended a teen rally in town. The speakers spoke appealingly about the love of God, and Terry made a decision to ask Christ into her heart. For the first time she felt an overwhelming sense of love and knew she needed to somehow appropriate that love to her mother. Even though her mother rarely attended to Terry's emotional needs, Terry was determined to try and connect with her.

As she studied the Bible, she was increasingly moved by the words of Christ to love her mom despite the years of neglect. For months Terry smiled and told her mother she loved her. She did her best to bestow on her mother the Christlike love that she cherished so much herself.

Then Terry met a young man in her church group, and they started dating. Both were committed to sexual abstinence based on their new spiritual commitments. Terry's mother, however, began to tease them about their stance. She provided birth control and told her daughter to stop being a religious prude. Daily, she ridiculed Terry for being uptight and religious. If she could only loosen up and party, she said, they could be friends.

Terry held her position; yet she did not respond to her mother's teasing by pulling away from her. Instead, she talked about the joy she now experienced—a better high than her mom could ever find through drugs and alcohol. Terry prayed for her mother and asked God to help her be Christ to her mom and to love her mother unconditionally. As she did, the relationship began to change. Terry's mom saw the genuine happiness in her daughter, and she wanted what Terry had. Slowly, she began questioning Terry about her new faith.

Terry's hope was in Christ, not in her mother. She asked God to put a supernatural love for her mother inside her, and He did. Then her loving response began to change her mother's heart. In this case, Terry took the lead in making a needed change. She found a source of strength outside her messed-up family, and she used it to overcome the dysfunctional-family influences that could have pulled her under.

Because we are in relationship with God, and because God promises to restore, redeem, and make us new—no matter how tangled our pasts—we have hope that our restlessness can be calmed, that our unworthiness can be turned to value, and that our lack of acceptance can be replaced by unconditional love and favor. God, the best parent and the only parent incapable of failing us, is always available. He is love. He is our hope.

GROWING SPIRITUALLY AND RELATIONALLY WITH GOD—AND OTHERS

A daughter needs to understand whose image she reflects as she attempts to separate and form her own identity. Yes, she is her mother's daughter and a reflection of that image, but she is also the daughter of the Creator—beautifully and wonderfully designed. Through the spiritual bond, she emerges as a reflection of the crowning glory of God in creation. Her identity, though formed in the context of earthly relationships, is ultimately found in Christ. Apart from Him, she searches for acceptance and approval.

No matter what our family struggles may be, God is with us, loving us, caring for us, and esteeming us so that we can accomplish His purpose and plan for our lives. He wants the best for us.

So whatever your earthly circumstances, there is hope for you because you are a daughter of the Most High. You have a spiritual position of royalty. You are accepted and loved. And this status is not based on anything you do, but only on being God's child.

But we, His daughters, must choose to be and stay in relationship with Him. It is in the context of this relationship that we grow and define ourselves. As we discover our true identity in Christ, we are released to be our true selves. If we wander away and try to find our identity through other people or other things, we'll miss the mark.

If you choose to work on your relationship with God, you will grow spiritually and relationally. Then, even in the most difficult earthly relationship, you can learn to respond with maturity. And a merciful and graceful response may open up new relationship possibilities, as it did for Terry.

Leaving Home but Staying Connected

Reading through the Gospels, I am always reminded of how Jesus called His disciples to leave their mother and father and follow Him. I used to think, *How insensitive. Why does He have to be so abrupt and make them choose? Can't they go back home and at least tell their families their plans? One guy couldn't even bury his father!*

But I now understand the importance of Christ's message. He called these men to be with Him to do His work after He returned to heaven. The time was short and the mission too important to waste even a day. He didn't have time for them to go home and work through their family's reaction. Soon He would be sending them out alone, and He knew they would have to stand on their own and be persecuted for His sake. So He wanted to deposit all He could in them before His departure. Time alone with His disciples was vital to their survival and the survival of the early church. He was calling them out to be separate, yet to be their own person in relationship to Him.

Mothering is like that. Mothers want to deposit all they can in their daughters before they send them out into the world to accomplish all God has for them. Daughters need to be ready to survive under fire and to stand for goodness and righteousness. They learn to do this in relationship with God and with their family, especially with their mother. And mothers only have a short time to accomplish this mission.

So what does it really mean to "separate" from our mother? Is this some form of finding ourselves, navel gazing, or sitting on a mountaintop and humming mantras into space? Do we need to spend years in therapy working through our early unconscious experiences in order to separate from our mother? I hope not! Speaking for myself, I know my navel is pretty boring, and my insurance won't permit years of psychotherapy!

Separation is defining yourself as an individual. It's becoming the unique person God intended you to be. It's not a single act but a continuum, a process that takes a lifetime as you learn to be your authentic self while staying connected to God and others, in this case, your mother.

Where are you on this continuum of separation? Are you able to take a position that differs from your mother's, be your true self, express your opinions, have your own thoughts, and make your own decisions? Or are you living with guilt, anger, bitterness, unforgiveness, anxiety? Are you cut off, emotionally distant, and yet unable to have a thought of your own?

We all have to leave home at some point—at least that is the hope! Yet too many of us haven't even packed our bags. Or we packed angry bags years ago and never looked back. We are still waiting for Mom to be the perfect mother she was supposed to be, and we won't reconnect until we've experienced her in some idealized way. Or we've convinced ourselves that we don't need her. Either way, we live in denial. Being cut off is not autonomy.

False Starts

I'm not much of a race fan, but I do know that when horses race, they need to come out of the gate right or they can have what is called a "false start." A false start happens when the horse gets a jump on the gun or does something the rules don't allow.

Leaving home can be a lot like one of horse racing's false starts. In order to run on the track of independence, the way you leave the gate makes a difference. Independence that begins with a false start creates problems in the race of life. Let me explain.

As I said, everyone, at some point in their life, is supposed to grow up, leave home, and be on their own. However, this doesn't mean you wave good-bye and never look back. It simply means there comes a time in your life when you jump into the water from the family boat and begin to swim using your own arms.

For most Americans, independence takes its first big step after high school with a decision to move out and get a job or go to college or enroll in some type of further schooling or job training. In our culture, leaving home is a developmental step toward autonomy.

In a healthy family, leaving home is something for which you have gradually prepared. Within your family, you practice taking steps of autonomy and develop a sense of who you are. You are given responsibility and included in decision making. When the time for leaving comes, you feel as prepared as you can be. There is no need to run away or feel guilty for not staying. You don't have to escape into numbing drugs or alcohol or pretend things are different. You and Mom function on a personal, intimate level. You have stretched your new wings of independence and found them a little scary but exciting. You understand that you can become your own person and still be in relationship with Mom and the rest of your family. In fact, you count on checking in for continued guidance.

In contrast, for those daughters who feel unprepared, the prospect of leaving home can be frightening and anxiety provoking. If you don't feel ready to take on the challenges of this new developmental time, you may try to stall the process. Rather than face the uncertainty of your growing independence, you may find yourself entangled in teen pregnancy, drug and alcohol use, eating disorders, depression, anxiety attacks, and other conditions that create a continued but unhealthy dependence on the family. And these problems delay your personal growth.

Unable to appropriately lunge out of the gate, you falter at the start. You hate your dependence but fear your independence. How can you resolve this problem? The answer has everything to do with achieving a good balance between being your own person and being a daughter. Here are three problems that can affect your autonomy:

1. The Overinvolved Daughter

Independence frightens you, so you never really leave home. You live near your mom, make frequent visits, call her every day, and have no social life apart from your family. You check with your mom for every decision and think more about how she is doing than about how you can increase your independence. You have no "self" apart from Mom and the family.

As ironic as it seems, you may even get pregnant and have children, not as a stalling tactic, as mentioned earlier, but out of a fear of independence. By having your own children, you can pour all your energy into them so you don't have to think about your own life issues. Your whole life revolves around taking care of your children. They become the source of all gratification and identity, a great distraction from knowing yourself.

Or you may stay close to Mom because you are simply afraid to launch out on your own. The family is safe, and you know what to expect.

Mary was one of those fearful young women. She felt unprepared to tackle life outside the confines of her family. I was scheduled to see Mary for an eating-disorders evaluation. Usually I see the entire family during the evaluation, and at Mary's evaluation, I began to ask her questions, but she didn't answer a single one of them. Instead, every time I directed a question to twenty-five-year-old Mary, her mother answered for her. When I repeatedly asked her mother to be silent, she refused and continued to answer for her daughter while Mary sat passively, looking hopeless and overpowered.

On the day of her next appointment, my secretary called and told me that Mary had arrived and was ready to be seen. When I walked out to the waiting room to retrieve her, I couldn't find her. "Where is she?" I asked the secretary.

"She's here," the secretary replied. "She came with her mother. I heard her tell her mother she had to go to the bathroom. Then I saw the mother follow her into the bathroom. They're both still in there . . . together."

Sure enough, I knocked on the door of the single-commode

bathroom, and both mother and daughter were inside. The mother's voice rang out, "Just a minute. She's almost ready." The door opened wide, and they both stood there. The daughter looked embarrassed, almost childlike, and the mother pushed her toward me. I didn't need to further evaluate. I'd already made my diagnosis: joined at the hip.

2. The Superficial Daughter

Perhaps you've physically left home and are making efforts to be independent, but your relationship with mom is superficial. You visit at the right times and remain the dutiful daughter, but little is shared in terms of your emotional and relational life. There is no real closeness. You feel mature, but this maturity is not based on intimate connections because you have decided to stay safe and keep your feelings and opinions hidden. Visits involve reports of success, basic facts about your recent activities, and the weather. As long as you can make small talk about your job, your boss, your husband or children, the relationship is comfortable.

Rita was a superficial daughter. She prided herself on being able to avoid personal subjects with her mom. "Let's just say that my mom and I do best when we avoid any talk about ourselves. When I'm with her, I don't want to get into the things that bother me, and she doesn't want to bring up any conflict. We've found a way to be together that works for both of us. We keep things at a surface level."

"Rita, do you find this relationship satisfying?" I asked her. "And do you think it influences how you are with other people? How about your girlfriends? Are you close with them, or do you see this pattern of superficiality repeating itself in your other relationships?"

"I wish I had a closer relationship with my mom. I do feel like I am missing something," she admitted. "As a matter of fact, I'm not close with anyone, but right now I don't see that as a problem. I have a career to think about. I'm focusing all my energy on the job."

"Any conflicts with bosses?"

"Well, yes, but I don't see how that relates to my mom," she said. "You don't have to be close to bosses or employees. You just go in and do your job and hope they don't get mad at you."

"Has that worked?"

"Not always. Right now they are upset with me, but I'm hoping it will all blow over."

What Rita failed to recognize was that her lack of intimacy with her mother translated to her work relationships as well. Instead of solving problems and dealing with differences, Rita just stayed superficial with her mom, hoping to avoid any real conflicts. Because she never practiced intimacy skills, she didn't know how to resolve problems when they arose elsewhere, including at her job. So when a work problem erupted, she simply hoped it would blow over, taking the same approach she used with her mother.

But work environments, like families, don't always allow you to stay superficial. Working day in and day out with a boss requires relationship skills that move beyond superficiality. If Rita would work on moving beyond superficiality with her mom, her work relationships would also improve. Or, Rita could work on solving problems with her boss, and her relationship with her mother would improve. Both relationships required more of Rita than maintaining a superficial façade.

3. The Cut-Off Daughter

You've decided that the only way you can truly be yourself is to cut yourself off from family contact and do your own thing. This way, no one will question you or cause you to feel upset. You rarely if ever call your mom, and contact is nonexistent. You feel independent because you don't have to deal with your crazy family. This is a false sense of independence because is it based on being cut off, not on relating. Being cut off feels safe and protective because you have temporarily removed yourself from the source of conflict or pain.

"My family is just crazy," Judy told me. "I can't be around them. When I am, I start to feel crazy too. My dad is verbally abusive, and my mom is as passive as a washcloth. She sits and takes all his garbage and lives a very depressed life. I couldn't wait to get out of there and leave it all behind. It's depressing. I don't really want anything to do with those people. They may be related to me, but I don't like them. I'm on my own now, so I don't have to deal with them."

"Oh, but you do," I told her. "Maybe not physically, but they are with you wherever you go. You can find a way to reconnect, or you can pretend none of it matters and run away. If you don't reconnect in some way that's safe for you, you'll replicate those cut-off patterns in other relationships, including your marriage or your friendships."

THE WAY YOU COME OUT OF THE GATE MATTERS. If you haven't "left home" in a healthy way, the repercussions will be felt in other relationships. The goal of this book is to show you it is possible to reconnect with Mom if you are cut off. There are ways to rebalance your priorities if you are overinvolved or to move into a more intimate relationship if you are superficial. If you've had a false start out of the gate, then, in the words of family therapist James Framo, "You can, and indeed, should go home again."[1] Keep reading!

THOUGHT POINTS

1. How much of your true self do you let your mother see? What parts do you hide from her?

2. Who or what else in your life influences your attempts to become your own person?

3. List some good and not-so-good characteristics about your mother. Make a choice to focus on the positive points of connection you have with her.

4. Did you leave home in a healthy way? If not, what do you need to change in order to leave home (emotionally) well?

Families: The Ties That Define

MAY I SEE THE HAND of anyone who came from what you would call a functional family? Of course, no one reading this is raising her hand. OK, maybe one or two of you are. But you are probably living in denial! Family therapists joke that if we ever held a conference for functional families, no one would attend! Functional or dysfunctional, it's all a matter of degree.

Gail expressed what some of you may feel. "It's so unfair. Why was I born into this horrible family? My father sexually abused me from the age of eight until I ran away from home at sixteen. My mother was depressed and mentally ill. My older brother got involved in a gang, and my younger brother is a drug addict. When I watch TV shows, I wish my family was just a little like those on the screen. We are such a mess."

Dysfunctional families seem to be everywhere. Women like Gail have a full plate of dysfunction. Others deal with minor annoyances. The point is, no family is perfect. And no mother is perfect. But how you respond to her imperfections and the family dysfunction is what matters.

You are born into a family system. This is a fact over which you have no control. You get what you get, and it forever influences you. This may not seem fair. But it also isn't a death sentence.

Women like Gail have a lot of baggage to unload because of their upbringing, but they can learn to unload it. Other women create family problems because of bad choices they make and have to learn to take responsibility for their choices. Still other daughters come from fairly healthy families but are negatively influenced by outside forces. The family unit may be functioning well but the surrounding community and culture aren't. As therapist Mary Pipher points out, families may be functional but often have to contend with living in "dysfunctional communities" that negatively influence their daughters.[1]

Perhaps you feel your upbringing was fairly healthy, but you still struggle to let go of past hurts. Whatever the case, making peace with Mom entails sifting through your family "stuff" in order to emerge sane and healthy in your current relationships.

Why are families such hard work? Because families are the most powerful emotional system to which we belong. You can't ignore your family and hope it will go away. Your family members are like fictional ghosts, constantly haunting you if you don't deal with them. Even when you no longer live with your original family, it is with you.

In addition, our family, no matter how healthy or unhealthy, helps form our sense of identity; it is the emotional playground of learning. Families can be pressure cookers of stress, places of nurturing and healing, or systems of hurt and abuse.

As we move through the family life cycle, we learn about intimacy and relationships. Since women tend to define themselves through relationships, our attachment and affiliation to our mother matters—a lot! The healthier our family relationships, the healthier the mother-daughter bond. The more dysfunctional the family, the more problematic the daughter emerges.

FAMILY LEGACIES

Family therapists Ivan Bosozormenyi-Nagy and D. Ulrich talk about the importance of family legacies. They say legacies are the life goals and values that get passed from generation to generation through your family. These legacies can be obvious or subtle, but they affirm the family and are emotionally laden. Family legacies influence and motivate our life choices.[2]

In order to better understand your family, it helps to be aware of these generational obligations that are passed down to you. Most legacies are adaptive and supportive and bring a sense of continuity to families. However, family legacies and loyalties can also be unhealthy. For example, there may be family legacies that insist it's unsafe to talk about abuse or that ignore Mom's drinking problem. There may be attitudes that imply, "You won't disagree with me or there will be hell to pay," or "You will marry someone of money," or "You won't vote Republican." In many cases, daughters feel bound to carry out these handed-down obligations. When they can't do so, or when they feel ambivalent about them, problems can arise.

In my family, one legacy was that you must go to college in order to have a successful life. The expectation was so ingrained that when I graduated from high school I didn't even know there were other options. Education is highly valued and a desired life goal. If one of the three children in my family had chosen not to go to college (all of us did), we would have "let down" the family. We all felt the pressure to do well academically and fulfill the expected family legacy. There were no problems related to this obligation because we all fulfilled it.

And frankly, we are all happy we did. But what happens when your life choices conflict with family legacies? In a word, problems.

For example, Holly came to me for a problem with depression. Her mother owned her own business—a woman's clothing store—and both her brothers worked for the company. As the only daughter, Holly was expected to take over the business when her mother retired. Holly, however, had little interest in becoming a businesswoman and preferred a more traditional role as a wife and mother. When she tried to discuss her wish to marry and become a stay-at-home mom, her mother wouldn't hear of it. Instead, Mom reminded her that she was a college graduate and needed to use her degree for "something more meaningful than staying home." According to Mom, Holly's loyalty was first to her family. Holly was expected to become a career woman like her mother. If she became a wife and more traditional mother instead, she would be considered disloyal.

Exhausted from emotional combat with her mom, Holly's depression worsened. She struggled with guilt and wondered if she was being selfish. Ambivalence characterized her thoughts. Should she do what she felt was best, given her desires, or should she give in to the family pressure and head the company? Maybe her legacy was not motherhood but carrying on the family business. Nothing inside her wanted to run a business, but seeing the incredible disappointment in her mother's eyes week after week was too much to bear. Her depression was rooted in a problem of family legacy. How could she be loyal to Mom and still fulfill her own dreams?

How many of our complaints about our mom are embedded in our need to please her and be loyal to family legacies? It is hard work to grow up and be true to self. We won't always find agreement. Understanding the power of family legacies can help you figure out if you struggle with an issue of family loyalty. As an adult daughter, are you still looking for your mother's approval and acceptance in all you do? If so, it's time to take up your positions and decide what's true for you regardless of what the family thinks. This doesn't mean you will always be at odds with your family. Chances are there will be many times of agreement, but on those occasions when you know differently, take your stand.

One faction of my extended family members used to make fun of me for pursuing graduate studies in social work. While in college, I was called the family "do-gooder" and mocked by them at family dinners. I admit, I became very upset by this, but I didn't let it dissuade me from my choice of field. I believed (and still do) that social work was compatible with my Christian faith. Jesus tells us to care for the poor, to help the brokenhearted, to set free those bound in prison, and to help the less fortunate. Social work has this core value. I understood that these extended family members disagreed with how that mandate should be carried out. Despite the political arguments we had, I stayed my course.

On more difficult matters, I have watched many women heal from abuse because they refused to keep destructive family secrets. Their decision to confront the family silence put them in a lonely place when they dared to challenge the unhealthy legacy of abuse. One woman I treated endured the silent treatment from her entire family for three years because she decided to confront the incest in the family. Even though she and all her sisters were victims, for many years no one would break the silence. When she finally did, it got ugly. But she has healed because of it.

Maybe you don't have big family secrets or huge issues of loyalty, but you have that nagging feeling that when you are with your mom, you are not being true to self.

For example, have you ever had that experience of staying in your childhood bedroom as a grown woman and feeling like you are ten years old again? Away from that bedroom, you seem like a competent adult woman. But once you set foot in that house, you revert to that little child. And you find yourself responding to your mom in those old ways. If you want to feel differently, you have to make changes, not in your mom but in your reactions to her.

DANCING WITH MOM

Harriet Lerner, in her helpful book *Dance of Anger*, explains how all relationships are made up of dances. You make a move, then the other person makes a move. Then you react and she reacts. The process is like a dance in which each of you takes specific steps. I love the metaphor because it is so visual in helping us understand that all relationships involve these dance steps. Most of the time we are so busy trying to change the steps of our dance partner that we rarely think of our own steps in the dance.

This is definitely true with mothers and daughters. We have developed familiar dances with our mom. She makes a move, we make a move, then she makes another move, and so the dance goes. If you don't like the current dance, change your steps!

Here's how it works. Your mother calls and criticizes you about your parenting. You react angrily and criticize back. Then she yells even louder, and you angrily hang up the phone. Not a great dance, so you decide to change it.

The next time she begins criticizing you, you take a new step. You tell her how hurt that criticism makes you feel. Change doesn't always happen immediately, so she continues the criticism in an attempt to get you to go back to the familiar dance. (You are supposed to criticize back.) Instead you stand firm and say, "Mom, I just told you how much that hurts." Bewildered, she stops. Now the dance is different. You didn't tell her to change; you changed your step.

If you feel like a little girl with your mother, try stepping out of that childhood dance and taking some grown-up steps. Expect resistance when you change your dance. Change is unfamiliar, and people tend to resist it, even when it's change for the better.

YOUR MOTHER, YOURSELF

Family patterns get transmitted down the generations. Both deliberately and subconsciously, mothers teach their daughters what it means to be female—a wife, a sister, an aunt, a working woman, a daughter, or any other role she may hold. Behavior and values are learned and passed from generation to generation.

Messages may be spoken or unspoken. For example, a spoken rule in our house is that children are to check with both parents for permission to do something. We don't believe in the divide-and-conquer strategy when it comes to saying yes or no to an activity. This rule carries an unspoken message to my daughter that women have equal say, equal power, in parenting. You don't go to Dad to undercut Mom. Dad values Mom. I am influencing her ideas about being female. In this case, I am not teaching her to manipulate men to get what she wants. She sees Mom as an equal force with which to contend. And she is influenced by that model.

I was influenced by the same model in my family. I saw my mom as an equal and valued partner by my dad. When she said no, she meant it, and there wasn't any behind-the-scenes manipulating of one parent against the other. They were a team. My daughter sees that pattern repeating in our family today. I hope she will feel empowered as a wife and mom one day.

Patterns of relating are passed down the generations through various ways. One of those ways is simply how you live your life. It's called modeling. For example, if you solve problems through anger, you'll teach those in your family to do the same. If you model healthy behavior and values, that's what you will teach your family.

As family therapist Betty Carter once said, "The most important legacy a mother gives her daughter is the way she lives her own life—and the kind of relationship she conducts with her own mother."[3] This is a powerful and sobering statement. In other words, it's not what mothers say that counts the most; it's how they actually live their lives. One of the things your daughter is seeing is how you deal with your mom—just one more reason to strengthen that intimate connection.

DIVIDED LOYALTIES

The pull you often feel toward your family has to do with issues of loyalty. When we were children, our parents were charged with caring for us and being responsible for us. To the extent that they were successful in earning our trust, we feel indebted to them. Our repayment, as family therapist Bosozormenyi-Nagy says, is our loyalty. Children usually feel some level of obligation to their parents for raising them.

The dilemma for mother-daughter pairs comes when the pull for family loyalty conflicts with the daughter's individual values, life goals, or needs. A daughter is always trying to balance this divided loyalty. What does she owe her parents? How much can she pull away and do her own thing without feeling guilty? Many women who feel they were unloved or unjustly treated spend their adult lives trying to balance issues of loyalties. Often the unresolved feelings they have toward their mother are played out with husbands or intimate partners.

Here's the lesson from this fact: you can't assume your rightful position as a grown-up daughter when you take the position of victim. When you continue to blame Mom for what she did or didn't do, you are still looking for her approval and acceptance. You may never get it. If you don't, the way to resolve the problem is to grieve the loss, find this acceptance elsewhere, and move on with your life.

FAMILY TRIANGLES

A family triangle is not difficult to understand, but it is important. Think of the three sides of a triangle. One side is you; the other two sides are two other people in your family. Triangles happen in a family when two people stop relating directly and a third party comes into the picture to reduce the resulting tension or anxiety. While this third person stabilizes the interaction, he or she does so by diverting the interaction away from the original two people; they don't resolve the issue between themselves. When triangles form under stress, problems can erupt.

Here's an example of how a "triangulation" problem can occur. Mary and Tom are divorced and fight over the curfew they will set for their sixteen-year-old daughter Courtney. Every time Mary tries to get Tom to agree on an earlier curfew time, Tom puts Courtney on the phone to plead her case. Tom and Courtney form two sides of the triangle against Mary. Now the argument is no longer between the two parents, as it should be. Courtney has been "triangulated" into the disagreement. Courtney sides with Dad against Mom—an unhealthy triangle.

Here's another example. Deidra is very upset with her mom for missing her children's piano recital. Deidra has problems telling her mom when she is angry. Using an old pattern, she tells her dad how upset she is. Her dad then talks to her mom and describes Deidra's upset. The mom feels bad. Deidra's dad relates his wife's feelings to Deidra. Deidra is in an unhealthy triangle with her dad against her mom. She hasn't learned to directly resolve a problem with her mom and instead aligns with her dad against her mom. Her father fights her battle while Deidra remains distant from her mom. The original conflict is between Deidra and her mom. Dad is triangulated into the problem.

Another situation shows how a family member opted out of the triangle. The problem in Nancy's case was that her mother constantly complained to her about her father. After her parents' divorce, Nancy's mom began to spill all her dissatisfaction with her ex-husband on Nancy. At first, Nancy felt she should listen in order to give her mom support. But as the criticism continued, Nancy noticed the negative effect this criticism was having on her relationship with her dad.

After talking about the problem in therapy, Nancy told her mom that she no longer wanted to hear her mother's complaints about her father. She explained how her mom's intimate complaints about Dad put her in a difficult position. Nancy still maintained a relationship with Dad and didn't want it tainted by Mom's complaints. She was not unsympathetic to her mother's pain, but she couldn't be the sounding block for it. Nancy wanted out of the triangle, especially since the reasons for the divorce had little to do with her.

The problem with triangles is that they prevent people in a family from dealing with each other person to person. In the case of mother-daughter relationships, the more distance there is between a mother and daughter, the more a third party will be triangulated into the relationship. Here's an example: Madison and her mom were emotionally distant from one another and rarely saw each other despite living in the same town. Every year, Madison wondered if her mom wanted to be included in her holiday plans but never asked her directly. Instead, she had her sister pump Mom for information about her plans. Based on her sister's reports, Madison would either ignore Mom during the holidays or invite her to dinner. The distance between Madison and Mom was bridged by the sister, the third part of the triangle. This "triangulation" prevented Madison from developing a more meaningful relationship with her mom. Getting her sister out of the triangle would require Madison to directly ask her mom about her holiday plans and wishes.

When mothers and daughters are overly close, triangles often serve to prevent direct communication with other family members. For example, Sonja felt she had to check every decision she made with her mom. When she and her husband decided to purchase a new car, Sonja called her mom to see if she approved. This infuriated her husband. "Why do you have to check with your mother? What does she have to do with our decision to buy a new car?" he screamed.

"See, I can't talk to you," Sonja replied. "You wouldn't understand. I trust my mom's advice."

"You don't trust me?" her husband yelled.

"I really don't want to talk about this," Sonja sobbed.

In this example, Sonja had a trust problem with her husband but wasn't dealing with him directly. Instead, she sought her mom's advice. Sonja's mother was happy to give advice and reassured her daughter to trust and come to her whenever she needed wisdom. The mother was undermining the couple's relationship, and Sonja was allowing it. This triangle prevented Sonja and her husband from working out their trust problems. Without Mom, Sonja would have to talk to her husband.

Daughters can be involved in family triangles with their mother and father, their mother and grandmothers, their sisters and other family members. Triangles can happen anytime two people don't deal with each other directly.

When you're involved in a triangle that is causing problems, the work is to detriangulate yourself from these unhealthy threesomes. In other words, get out of the middle and develop a person-to-person relationship with each member of your family. Sometimes you can do this by simply acknowledging the triangle. This was the case in the following example.

A family was in therapy because the adult daughter was bulimic. She was married and had a younger brother who still lived at home. The father was very controlling and the mother extremely passive. There was obvious marital tension that was never acknowledged by anyone in the family.

During our sessions, I noticed that the mother always sat by her son. He would whisper to her but never say anything out loud during the session. The women (the mother and her adult daughter) were too frightened of the dad to speak, and the son-in-law knew his place, given the dad's history of punishing remarks for questioning his authority.

There were several unhealthy triangles operating in the family. The adult bulimic daughter only spoke to her mother and avoided her father. She coped with the emotional loss of her father by bingeing and purging. The high school son was depressed and not doing well in school. He spoke only to his mother no matter who upset him.

At one point, I turned to the son and asked how it felt to be married to his mother. Stunned by the question, the mother and father were horrified that I had made such an analogy. The father threatened to walk out of the session if I didn't take my question back. But the mother watched me carefully when I didn't back down from him or my question and asked the son again. With a sign of relief, the son spoke, "I'm tired of being my mom's confidant. I don't want the job, and I understand why my sister throws up. Hey, I'm just a kid. They [Mom and Dad] need to work out their problems without me in the picture."

With those words, the son was asking to step out of the triangle involving his mother and dad. Soon after he spoke, the daughter piped up, "Dad, it's hard to talk to you. Look at what you did to Dr. Mintle." She was trying to triangulate me into the conversation.

"You need to speak for yourself," I suggested. "I'll deal with your dad on my own." I was removing myself from the triangle.

"OK, well, I, too, am tired of always talking to Mom when I am really upset with you, Dad," the daughter said. "Can you stop being so mean? Like when we leave here today, what will you do to all of us for even bringing this up? You'll yell at us and threaten us, and then no one will say anything again. So we never resolve problems. I swallow my upset, and then vomit it out. Frankly, I'm tired of throwing up over it."

The triangles were exposed, and the work to detriangulate began. Daughter, son, and mother each had to deal with Dad on his or her own terms. Fortunately, when every member of the family spoke up, Dad realized he had a problem and even apologized to me!

This story also illustrates a common triangle: father/mother/daughter. In many of these families, the parents haven't learned how to disagree or handle conflict, so the daughter gets triangulated into the marital relationship. The parents may become overly concerned about the daughter and focus on her as a way to come together. This happens frequently in families with a daughter who has an eating disorder. Tension and stress characterize the marital relationship, and the daughter's eating disorder brings the parents together for a mutual cause: the well-being of the daughter. Anxiety and arguments are focused on the daughter and not the marriage. This pattern helps the parents successfully avoid marital conflicts, and the daughter avoids her need to become more autonomous.

If you are in an unhealthy triangle with your mother, you need to get out of it and encourage the two people with the problem to deal with one another directly. Or if you don't speak to your mom directly without bringing someone else into the picture, work on getting the other person out of the picture and deal with your mom directly.

In order to stop unhealthy triangles from forming, think about your family relationships. Who do you have difficulty dealing with directly? Do you bring in a third party? If so, try to address the person with whom you have the issue directly. Furthermore, if you are in an unhealthy family triangle, refuse to side with one of the two parties. Ask the other two people to deal with each other directly. Stay out of the middle. This will feel uncomfortable at first, and you may feel a pull to be dragged back into the middle, but resist.

Repeating Patterns

Another helpful strategy is to begin to identify the unhealthy patterns passed down to you that negatively impact your relationship with your mom. For example, are you quick to be angry, critical, blaming—ready to jump on any failure or mistake? Do you avoid conflicts? Do you ask for help when you really don't need it? Are you too distracted with life to visit or call your mom or other family members? Do you see any of these patterns repeating in other family members?

Here's an example of how these negative patterns can be repeated in subsequent generations. Becky felt like a lost child growing up. She was the youngest of four children, and it seemed her mom never had time for her. When Becky tried to get Mom's attention, Mom was too busy washing clothes, ironing, cooking, or running errands. Becky's oldest sister basically raised her.

As Becky got older, she noticed her mom always seemed over-whelmed with life—on the edge and stressed. Mom complained that there was never enough time in the day to do everything she needed to do. At the end of the day, she retreated to her room, exhausted.

Becky noticed that this pattern was repeating in her own life. Even though she had only two children, she felt similar to her mom. And she worried that her two daughters would grow up resenting her lack of attention, as she had done during her childhood. How could this happen when Becky remembers hating this situation as a child? It happened because Becky learned how to cope with stress from her mom. The pattern was repeating, and Becky came to therapy to learn how to be less compulsive about completing her never-ending work so she could enjoy spending more time with her daughters.

Patterns repeat whether or not you are aware of them. Even when you are aware as Becky was, it takes work to escape the pattern. The good news is that you can unlearn a bad habit or a negative pattern. It just takes intention, time, and practice.

First you must identify what needs to be changed. What are those generational patterns that you find yourself repeating? Think about the TV family, the Osbournes. They are a classic example of generational patterns repeating. The first time you heard the profanity coming out of daughter Kelly, you may have been speechless, but when you learned that the mother, Sharon, also has a filthy mouth, it came as no surprise. Like mother, like daughter. Sharon, the mom, admits that her use of cursing and objectionable language gives her children permission to do the same.

But remember. You don't have to be a victim of whatever family patterns are passed on to you. You can make changes. Renee found this out as she worked in therapy. She and her mother were alike when it came to speaking up when there was a problem. Both were afraid to hurt anyone by saying what really needed to be said.

Since her father died, Renee had felt obligated to have her mother over for dinner every Sunday. Usually this wasn't a problem, but whenever she ran into a conflict, Renee was afraid to tell her mother not to come.

A Daughter's Journey Home

As we talked about her hesitancy to speak up, Renee realized that she rarely brought up controversial issues and constantly worried about hurting her mom's feelings. As she was growing up, she had seen her mom walk on eggshells around her dad, who had struggled with depression most of his life. Renee's mom coped with his chronic depression by hiding her upsets from him and internalizing her feelings. Now Renee did the same. It didn't feel safe to share problems or raise controversy. She learned not to burden her mother.

When Renee needed to cancel Sunday dinner with mom, she couldn't bring herself to do it, fearing it would hurt her mom's feelings. Not only was Renee feeling responsible for her mom (a feeling she had carried since childhood) but she was unable to confront even the simplest conflict.

With coaching, Renee learned to be more forthright. When there was a schedule conflict, she called her mom and explained the problem. Her mom was disappointed but understood. Even though this was a small issue, it represented the message Renee internalized generationally: women keep problems to themselves and don't burden others or rock the boat. This unspoken family rule had caused Renee a great deal of unnecessary distress. With help, she learned to address conflict directly and not be responsible for her mother's feelings. As a result, she found out her mother was stronger than she thought.

Keep in mind that we are also given healthy and helpful generational patterns. For example, when problems come, I know to turn to God and expect results. This was modeled in my family as I grew up. When my mother had cancer, we prayed and God healed. When my brother was killed, God comforted us as we turned to Him. When my other brother was in a coma after being hit by a car, we prayed and God saved him. So many times in so many circumstances I saw my parents turn to God for help. I learned to do the same.

When I struggled with infertility for seven years, I knew I had to trust God and hold on to His promises. It wasn't easy, but it was almost automatic because I had watched my parents live out their faith when I was a child. In our family, God was the foundation. His presence in our lives impacted our world-view, and while I had my moments of turning away from Him, I never completely left. Why? Because the generational patterns were ingrained. I had grandparents who sought the Lord on all accounts, parents who prayed and turned to God in times of trouble, and my own experiences of having God answer my prayers. The generational pattern was modeled—call on God, and He will help you. Live your life in His presence and "taste and see that the LORD is good."[4]

ROMEO, WERE HE NOT ROMEO CALLED

Linda Sue. Not exactly a classic northern name. It came from a girl my dad knew when he was in the navy. He liked her and liked the name. I admire my mom for going along with the idea. She must have felt very secure to name me after one of my dad's girlfriends! Names send messages.

In Shakespeare's *Romeo and Juliet*, Juliet realizes the power of a name when she says in the classic balcony scene, "What's in a name? That which we call a rose, by any other name would smell as sweet. So Romeo would, were he not Romeo called, retain that dear perfection which he owes without that title." Juliet finds herself in love with a man whose family name means he is off-limits. His name means "enemy" regardless of his "dear perfection."

Names and labels mean something in families. They are often ties to the past, a historical connection. My daughter's middle name, Elizabeth, is a family name passed down for generations. It reminds her that she's in good company with women who are strong and competent.

A Daughter's Journey Home

Who are you named after? Aunt Sally, who never did things the conventional way? Grandma Rosalind, who was feisty and considered the black sheep of the family? Aunt Delores, who was always sickly and a hypochondriac? More important, what was your mother's relationship with these women? How does she talk about them, and how does that translate to you?

Claire was tired of being compared to her cousin Louise. Louise had made a number of bad choices in her life and whenever Claire would mess up, her mother would say, "You are going to be just like your cousin Louise if you keep that up." This warning would infuriate Claire. She felt as if her mother was dooming her to become a problem adult, like Louise. But, like many daughters, Claire never really dealt with the issue; she just got angry.

Claire's mother was unaware of the resentment her comparison was creating. She simply hoped to motivate Claire to make good choices in her life. When Claire finally raised the issue with her mom, her mother was surprised by Claire's reaction. "I knew you got angry when I said it, but I figured it was motivating you. I never knew you resented me for saying it."

Names, labels, and family comparisons are powerful shapers and influencers. No one likes to be treated as an extension of someone else. You may have to address negative labels and names if they have gone unchecked and have created bad feelings. Talk to your mom about this if this has been an issue in the past or exists today.

SEEING THE BIG PICTURE—AND MAKING CHANGES

Once you become aware of unhealthy family triangles, negative patterns of relating, family legacies and loyalties, and the power of names and labels, you have a much broader picture of how these issues can impact your mother-daughter relationship. And now you know how to make changes.

Let's review:

1. Identify the unhealthy triangles that involve you and your mother. Detriangulate the third party and develop person-to-person relationships.

2. Identify any negative patterns in your mother-daughter dance and make a change in your responses. Your reaction to your mother matters and has the potential to bring about changes in your relationship.

3. Discuss family values, life goals, and expectations. Decide which ones you hold merely because you feel loyal to your family and which ones are true for you. If there are areas of ambivalence and anxiety, take a more self-defined position without becoming highly upset or overly distressed with your mom (more help for this is given in chapters 1, 2, and 8).

4. If you have held on to resentment or bad feelings because of labels or names you've been assigned, try talking about the impact of those labels with family members. Remember that while names and labels influence, they don't define our destiny.

The goal of this chapter has been to help you sort out the "stuff" of your family in order to improve your relationship with your mother. I hope you will now focus less on complaints and more on strategies for making changes. Define yourself and learn to control the part you play in your family interactions. *If you make changes in yourself, the family dynamics will change.* This should give you hope, even if you are the only person in your family who is motivated to change.

Your task is to come to terms with your original family, because, for better or for worse, those original relationship patterns replay in your adult relationships. You can't run away from them; they will play out again and again. If they are negative patterns and you choose not to address them, they will cause problems. I can't tell you the number of times I've seen marital problems related to ongoing struggles between mothers and daughters, fathers and daughters, or siblings. I tell my therapy clients, Deal with your family relationships now or watch them play out in other relationships. It's a choice you make, either deliberately or by default.

Even though families are fertile soil for mother-daughter relationships, as we'll see in the next chapter, other factors count too.

Thought Points

1. What generational patterns do you and your mom share? Identify both the positive and negative patterns. How can you begin to change your step in the dance?

2. Identify unhealthy triangles operating with your mom. What would it take to make changes?

3. Consider the power of names and labels in your family. How have these affected your feelings about yourself and impacted your relationship with your mom (or with other family members who have used the labels)? If possible, ask your mom if you were named after someone—and if so, ask how she feels about that person.

4. Have you felt pressured because of a perceived family legacy or loyalty? Consider what your alternatives are.

8

I Am My Mother—Not!

It's my favorite mug. Picture this: a shrieking woman pulling out her hair, looking totally stressed, and screaming, "Eeeeeeekkkkk. I AM my mother!" I laughed when I first saw it. Actually, its sentiment was funny, scary, and true, all at the same time. Yes, I am my mother. And so are you!

Years ago, this thought frightened me and I fought the idea. I loudly proclaimed, "I am my own person. Let me show you how different I am." Numerous women joined me in my naiveté. They told me so in therapy: "Listen, you need to know that I am nothing like my mother. In fact, I am the opposite of her."

When I heard this, I eyed these women with skepticism, knowing I had similar thoughts. But down deep, I sensed they weren't true.

What I finally realized was that I am my mother—and I am also a unique person. Both realities coexist. The sooner I understood this, the more work I could do on differentiating myself from her. I'm not her clone, but parts of her are alive and well in my breathing body.

A Daughter's Journey Home

Finding a balance between your individuality and your intimate connection with your mom takes some work. It requires getting a good handle on who you are in the relationship and not just focusing on how crazy she "makes" you feel. Don't be afraid to admit that you are like her in some ways. All daughters face this reality. Rather than deny or fear it, we need to embrace this. Why? Because it can be a good thing, and in order to make changes, you first have to admit there is something to change.

Because mothers and daughters have similarities, the emotional attachments between them can be intense and sometimes difficult to manage. Let's revisit our discussion about separation and attachment from a previous chapter. Remember how I talked about the daughter's need to grow up in a family and yet define herself separately from the rest of the family members? Your ability to define who you are and put your identity out there has everything to do with how well you resolve emotional issues with your mom.

We all have some degree of unresolved emotional attachments to our original families. And this degree of unresolved attachment is directly related to how well we see ourselves as a unique person in our family. Generally, the less we see ourselves as a different, unique person, the more unresolved emotional attachment we have with our parents. The more we react to every little thing our mom does that we don't like is usually a sign that we haven't developed a very good sense of who we are apart from her. And this lack of differentiating ourselves causes problems.

Developing the "I"

The way we deal with our anxiety over unresolved emotional attachments with our family, especially our mom, is influenced by whether or not we have a clear sense of ourselves. Do we know who we are?

Do we know what we think, feel, and believe to be true regardless of what others say?

As we mature, we struggle with these kinds of questions until, hopefully, we have some ideas. But many women never really develop a sense of themselves and then carry that undefined self into all their relationships. When this happens, problems emerge.

Daughters who are unclear about their individuality and have no "I" to reference have difficulty solving their emotional attachments to their mom. Usually they operate from one of two extremes. Either they use distance, both physical and emotional, to cope with relationship anxiety, or they have excessive closeness and are unable to define themselves apart from their families.

When you consistently react to your mom with strong emotions, it is because you aren't thinking from your own perspective. You haven't learned to establish appropriate boundaries and you don't assert yourself in the relationship. The reasons for this may be that you are afraid to express yourself or you don't know who you are or what you think apart from Mom.

When this happens, you may choose to avoid your mom. The problem with this strategy is that you'll end up recreating your mom in some other relationship. As soon as you experience stress and anxiety in "substitute" relationships, the pattern of distance will repeat. Then you'll look for a new relationship to replace the current one that isn't working. Nothing is solved.

So you might as well determine to work on unresolved emotional attachments with the original sources—your family and, for the purposes of this book, your mom.

Lisa's story illustrates this emotional attachment problem and how it can be resolved. For years, Lisa struggled to get along with her mother. She felt her mother was too controlling and that her mother squashed any individuality Lisa ever expressed. When she was eighteen years old, Lisa announced she was leaving home, moving into her own apartment, and getting a job. Her mother told her she wasn't ready for this step of autonomy and that she (Lisa) was too angry. Lisa blamed her mother for her anger and refused to work out a compromise. Her solution was to leave home and get away from her mother. This, she felt, was the step of independence she needed.

Six months later, Lisa was married and in a similar relationship with her husband. To no surprise, she married a man who was controlling and tried to direct her life. She had unconsciously found a substitute relationship for the unresolved issues with her mother.

A year later she was divorced and in a new relationship. This time, she dated a passive man with whom she became very controlling. Again, she was unhappy and hated the way she acted in this new relationship. But she felt as if she couldn't control her anger.

In therapy I pointed out that Lisa had married her mother and then, in her second relationship, she had become her mother.

Her mouth fell open.

I further explained that she was trying to work out her "mom tension" with men, and I suggested we go back to the original source of this unresolved tension and include her mother in our therapy work.

Lisa agreed. Time to bring in Mom and learn how to be her own person without having to oppose her mother. The work of therapy involved helping Lisa figure out what she thought, felt, and wanted out of life, not from a motive of rebellion but from a clear sense of who she was and what her life goals were. Then she had to learn to communicate her needs and wishes and set appropriate boundaries. She also had to realize that her mom might not cheer all her efforts because she might have different ideas.

Lisa calmly and firmly asserted her position on a number of issues. She apologized for being so rebellious and told her mom she wasn't pleased with many of her past decisions either. In the past, she acknowledged that she had opposed her mom just for the sake of exercising her independence. Now she was ready to make decisions based on her needs and beliefs, not out of rebellion.

After several mother-daughter sessions, Lisa's mom admitted that her need to control Lisa had been born out of fear. She had worried Lisa wouldn't "turn out right." Her rebellion was frightening to her mom, and she perceived it as a sign that she was a bad mother. She really didn't understand her daughter and that frightened her too. Now that Lisa wasn't so rebellious, she was ready to listen. Mom realized that the more she pushed Lisa to do things her way, the more Lisa rebelled. She promised to give her opinion when asked, and not tell Lisa what to do. All the time Lisa and her mom spent arguing with each other in Lisa's teen years prevented them from getting to know each other very well. Lisa's solution to cut off the relationship and move out furthered the divide between them. But once they had worked through their problems, not only did Lisa's relationship with her mother improve, but so did Lisa's choice of men. She dumped the new boyfriend and looked for a partner with whom she could have a healthier relationship.

Find Your Voice and Use It

Daughters must define who they are apart from the family—sometimes I say, apart from the family *mess*.

To do this, you have to get control over how you react emotionally to issues and to family members. Don't run from your mom or be so connected to her that you can't think for yourself. You need to strike a good balance between these two extremes.

As you begin to become a better observer of your family's dynamics and see the triangles operating and the part you play in the family patterns, you will respond less emotionally. Of course, you can never just observe your family, because you are a part of it. So you'll always have some times of emotional intensity with these intimate relatives. But you can learn to see the unhealthy patterns and reduce your times of upset and distress.

When you can stay involved over an emotional issue with your mom (that is, when you stay in touch with her and don't cut off the relationship because you disagree on something) and not feel like you have to defend your position, you have developed a sense of who you are apart from her. Let me explain. It's natural to defend your position when it differs from your mom's. Most of us want to explain why we feel or behave the way we do. When we do, we hope Mom understands and either agrees with us or validates our point of view. But when we state our opinion and Mom still disagrees, we don't have to get bent out of shape over the disagreement. We can love her and accept her right to see the world differently and not agree with our every thought. When we can take this nondefensive position, it means we have a sense of ourselves that doesn't disappear in our mother-daughter relationship.

It takes work to reach this point, but it's essential to your well-being that you do so. It's another part of what therapists mean when they refer to "finding your voice" (which means knowing what you think and feel and then lovingly expressing it). When you are confident about your voice, you don't get angry and defensive or feel the need to persuade others to agree with you.

Another story may help illustrate this point. Amy was a twenty-five-year-old daughter who married a man her mother didn't like. While Amy was dating her future husband, Amy's mom shared her concerns about this man. But Amy didn't want to hear them. The more her mom talked about the relationship problems she saw, the more Amy was determined to marry this man. Once she did, she began to have problems but wouldn't acknowledge them to her mom. Instead, she blamed her mother for not accepting her husband. Amy convinced herself that her problem was her mom's lack of support, not her own poor decision.

Once married, Amy's mother decided "what's done is done," and she began to focus on the positive attributes of Amy's husband. So when Amy became angry with her mother and accused her of being unsupportive, Mom was surprised. Down deep, Amy knew she had made a bad decision, but she wouldn't admit it to her mom or to herself. She couldn't tolerate the anxiety she felt knowing Mom was right, so she pushed her mom away by blaming her.

When Amy was finally able to see what she was doing, she confronted her mom. "Mom, I know you disagreed with my decision to marry this man. I did it anyway, and now I'm unhappy. I realize I was trying to blame you for my unhappiness and not take responsibility for my decision. I'm going to try and work on this marriage, but I'm also going to stop blaming you for my decision."

Amy's intense upset with her mom was based on two things:

First, she wanted her mom to agree with her choice of partner. When her mother didn't, Amy reacted emotionally: she got mad, cut off her relationship with her mother, and acted on her own. She couldn't tolerate her mother's different perspective because she was so busy being upset; she didn't stop and think about what was best for her. In relationships, we have to "own our feelings" while being open to feedback but not expecting others to always feel the same way. This catchy little phrase "own our feelings" means we need to be responsible for our feelings and stop blaming other people. No one makes us feel anything. Feelings are often a choice, fueled by our thoughts. We can control our emotions and not give in to anger, offense, and despair.

When Amy's mother disagreed with her, Amy couldn't handle the tension. Instead of facing the issue with her mother and learning more about her mother's view before she made her decision, Amy pushed her mother away. Amy's uncertainty about her own decision making was at the root of the problem. Amy really didn't know what she wanted and wasn't willing to admit that she didn't. Instead of being guided by her mom, who had more wisdom concerning marriage, Amy pretended to know what she wanted. In reality, she had no clue.

Second, Amy couldn't face the consequences of her own decision, so she tried to blame her mom. In this case, she used her mom's original negative feelings for Amy's husband (before she married him) as "kitchen sink" material to blame her. By "kitchen sink" material, I mean she threw in anything she could dredge up from the past to deflect the reality of the present. When Amy stopped judging her mother for her (justified) concerns and realized that her mother was now trying to support her decision, she admitted that she had behaved badly and was wrong to accuse her mom for all her problems.

The bottom line is, Amy wasn't ready to marry anyone. And she didn't want anyone else to point this out, especially her mother! So she tried to blame her mom, hoping that would deflect her unhappiness. Unfortunately, her decision resulted in emotional pain. She had been blind to the warning signs about the man that she, too, had seen but ignored while they were dating; she was rebelling against her mom and unable to define what she really wanted in a husband. In addition, she never thought about whether or not she was really ready for marriage. Instead, she was just reacting to (and trying to escape from) the emotional tension with her mom.

Amy admitted she chose to ignore problems when she saw them because she wanted to be independent. Her independence, however, was not based on her good sense or self-awareness. Instead it was rooted in rebellion against her mom. Becoming angry prevented her from working through her problems in a good way.

The better course would have been for Amy to allow her mom to say what she saw and then to accept and use that information as feedback from a more experienced adult who loved her and cared about her future. Then Amy could decide if she agreed with her mother's observations or not. But her rational thinking was overridden by her intense emotions.

Checking Your "I" Sight

So what does it mean to take an "I" position? Simply put, it means being true to self while relating to others. You can have your own opinion, think your own thoughts, and behave in ways you know to be right, and still love and relate to other people. You can decide what's right and true for you without becoming defensive, angry, and highly emotional. And you should always check your thoughts and actions according to God's Word.

If your parents didn't have a strong sense of their own identity and were easily influenced by family members, or if they were cut off from their family because they didn't know how to handle that relationship, you have probably learned to behave the same way. Let's face it. Families exert powerful influences. It's hard to always figure out what you think and feel when everyone has opinions. But you can work on it. You can learn to deal with family members without feeling like they run your life or without running away from them.

As a quick and easy way to assess your "I" sight, ask yourself these ten basic questions:

1. Do I have trouble taking a position without feeling guilty or angry if my mom doesn't agree with me?

2. Do I avoid tension with my mom and pretend she doesn't matter?

3. Do I do things for my mom that I resent and regret because I won't say no?

4. Do I not speak up because it would upset her or someone else in the family?

5. Am I afraid to be on my own; do I find myself constantly checking in with my mom for approval?

6. Do I even know what I think?

7. Do I care more about what my mom thinks than I do about discovering truth for myself?

8. Do I find myself making contact with my mom out of obligation rather than a meaningful relationship?

9. Do I feel like a totally different person away from my mom?

10. Do I do whatever my mom says, even when I disagree, because I am afraid I will lose her love?

If you answered yes to any of these questions, you have work to do when it comes to finding, developing, and practicing how to express your true self. In fact, the work you do with your mother will improve all your other relationships too. Sounds like worthwhile effort, doesn't it?

Achieving Balance

The key to dealing with your mother on any emotionally charged issue is to be able to take your position and hold it without becoming defensive or upset. You want to find a healthy balance between your need for her approval and your individuality. Whenever you and your mother disagree, try to handle it without getting so emotional that you either want to run away and not deal with her, or you give in to her position. If you do give in or run away from problems, you risk feeling angry, resentful, and alone.

Instead, consider these strategies for taking a position with your mom:

1. Don't try to get your mom on your team. Take your "I" position because it represents how you feel and think. There are times you may stand alone. I know this is tough to do because when you are uncertain, it's tempting to seek out others who agree with your position; their agreement reinforces you. Resist doing this. Instead, pray and think about what is right and how you should react to your mother's differing position. Consider what God has to say about your thoughts, attitudes, actions, and what you believe.

2. Change yourself. Be open to the feedback from your mom, but don't change simply because she tells you to. Change because you know it's needed. Instead of bucking under the pressure of what others say and do, use biblical standards to guide your behavior and make changes. As you grow in intimacy with God, your mom relationship will change for the better.

3. Don't underestimate your mom's reaction. Be aware that when you take an "I" position, your mom may try to influence you to change back to old patterns of going along with her wishes, even when they differ from your own. Familiarity is comfortable, and change is not. So if you go against her opinion or advice, she may react quite negatively. This happens in relationships all the time. But if you believe your position is true for you and not opposed to God's directives, don't give in to the negative reaction. Expect her to push you to go back to the old, familiar way of relating. When she does, stand your ground—without letting your emotions get the upper hand.

4. Be aware that strong reactions are a cue that you need to get a better perspective. If you find yourself reacting to something your mother says or does, and your reaction feels too intense for the moment—too "over the edge"—ask yourself, *Why am I getting so upset? Is my mom bringing up an issue that really bothers me? Do I know she's right and don't want to admit it? Do I hate having her point out a problem?*

5. Use planned distance to avoid impulsively reacting. If you find that when you try to deal with your mom, she becomes verbally abusive or critical and controlling, you may need a *planned* distance from her. This helps both parties cool down and gives you a chance to rehearse how you want to handle the situation and what you might want to say. Planned distance is obviously different from just cutting off or giving Mom the silent treatment. It is more like a grown-up time-out. It works like this: "Mom, this is getting too heated. I'm going to take a time-out. I need to calm down before we continue to talk." Or you might say, "Mom, I won't continue to talk to you when you say abusive things or yell or scream at me. I'll talk when you stop doing those things. Can we take a time-out?"

6. Deal with one issue at a time. If you have a long history of problems with your mom and the two of you seem to get into regular fights, try making changes one issue at a time. Take one minor problem and express your position without backing down. Be gentle but firm, no matter how she reacts. Then try dealing with another problem. Choose something that may be more important. Stay focused on the issue at hand and don't get into an argument. It takes two to argue. If you find yourself beginning to argue, stop and say, "Mom, I don't want to fight. Could we go back to the issue and see if we can agree on it or just agree to disagree?"

7. Write letters or practice with a chair. If you feel intimidated by your mother and fear you can't hold your own with her, start by writing letters, or practice how you would handle a difficult situation by talking to an empty chair in which you imagine she is sitting. Rehearsal can help you think ahead to how you might respond to emotionally difficult issues.

8. Change your routine. If you find yourself overly close to your mom (meaning, you aren't thinking for yourself) and feeling obligated to frequently call or visit, then change your routine so that your contact isn't so predictable and expected. This will help you feel less trapped. Your mom might complain about this, but don't give in to her complaining. Tell her that you love her but have a life apart from her. You have personal things to attend to that require your time. If she asks you what those personal things are, smile and say, "That's why they're called personal, Mom."

9. Decide how you feel about important issues. Most daughters don't just accept everything their mother tells them. As adult women, we have to decide what is true for us and live according to our defined standards. Think about your own views on all kinds of important subjects. Take the time to form your own opinion, asking God for wisdom and understanding and making sure your beliefs line up with His Word. For example, how do you feel about staying home with your children, about women who work outside the home, about putting your child in day care, or about running the household finances? Don't allow your mother to tell you how to feel; you decide. If the two of you are in agreement, great. If not, that's OK too.

10. Take responsibility for your own beliefs, actions, and feelings. Don't look for agreement or approval. It's great when it happens but not essential if it doesn't. You are responsible for you. No one makes you do or feel anything.

Intimate but Not Fused

Fusion is often confused with intimacy. Adult daughters desire to be close to their mom in intimate ways. We want to get to know them as women and hope they will know us as well. Fusion is something more than that. It moves beyond a desire for intimacy and is an extreme desire for completeness. In other words, you expect your mom to make up for all the hurt and upsets you feel in life. When she doesn't, you feel angry and disappointed.

When you are fused with your mom, you don't trust your own thinking and instead allow her to think for you and make her responsible for keeping you happy. This kind of fusion gives your mother power over your well-being. Because of this, you may try to constantly please and appease your mom.

Fusion is a form of emotional bondage. It will keep you stuck in any effort to define yourself as a unique person separate from your mother. Fusion is built on a false premise—that someone else could complete you. There is no such person. Only God can complete you. And He promises to make up the difference where others have let you down. So turn to God for completion, not to any human person. And learn to grieve the losses you have experienced with your mom. God is ready and willing to take on your hurts. His yoke is easy, and His burden is light.[1]

Too Much or Too Little

So how do you know if you are fused with your mom, too distant, or have a healthy connection? These questions may help you decide.

Fusion Questions

1. Do you talk to your mom about every issue in your current family?

2. Do you ask your mom what to do when it comes to making decisions versus making your own decisions?

3. When you try to think about yourself unrelated to your mom or family, do you draw a blank?

4. Do you feel like you need your family's support or you can't survive?

5. Do you side with your mom over your husband or other important relationships, even if she's wrong?

6. Do you have trouble saying no to your mom?

7. Do you need to talk with your mom daily or you feel stressed or guilty?

8. Are you constantly asking your mom to reassure you that you made the right decision?

9. If you're married, do you feel closer to your mom than to your husband?

10. Do you feel guilty having your own thoughts when they conflict with your mother's?

Distancing Questions

1. Do you stay away from your mom and avoid her?

2. Do you spend major holidays and family occasions without seeing or including your mom?

3. Do you avoid conflicts with your mom?

4. Do you walk away from your mom when things heat up and get tense, and so issues do not get resolved?

5. Do you try to show your mom how successful you are away from her?

6. Do you only have contact with your mom when there is a crisis?

7. Do you fantasize about having a different mother?

8. Do you keep your innermost thoughts and feelings hidden from your mom?

9. Do you pride yourself in your stance of pseudoindependence?

10. Are you carrying secret pain that involves your mom?

If you answered yes to most of these questions on either fusion or distance, you may need to rethink your relationship. Do you need to create more personal space or find ways to be more intimate? If so, here's how to begin:

First, identify your tendency to either pull away from your mom or be too fused. Be honest, using the questions above as a guideline.

Next, decide to take steps toward a healthy intimacy with Mom using the strategies below. Initially, these strategies may cause more problems because you are changing the old dance. But in the long run, you'll have a more genuine and authentic relationship. You'll know who you are, and you can work on making necessary changes.

Strategies to Overcome Distancing

If you find that your general reaction to tension and strain with your mom is to distance yourself from her, here are some strategies to help keep you from running away.

1. Purposely do an activity with your mom. Pick something you can do with your mom and make a date to do it. You might try a walk in the park, enjoy tea at a tearoom, go to a movie together, go shopping, play a game of cards, invite her over for dinner, share a sewing project, or work on a scrapbook together.

You may feel very uncomfortable doing anything with her because you haven't spent time with her in the past. That's OK; it gets easier the more you do it. Just determine to do it. You don't have to become her best friend, but if you never do anything fun or relaxing with her, it's difficult to address your relationship problems because all you have to work with are negative interactions. Create positive moments so your relationship has a healthy foundation on which to build.

2. **When there is a conflict, try to stay present and don't run away.** Your first impulse may be to run away, but try to stay in the situation when tension arises. You may need a ten-minute time-out (use that planned distance we talked about earlier) to cool down or you may need a few moments to take some deep breaths and pray, but resist the impulse to run away. The more you practice, the better you'll get at fighting the urge to run away.

3. **Work on your conflict-resolution skills** (see chapter 4). Sometimes we just don't know how to solve problems because we never saw problem-solving modeled as we were growing up. But problem-solving and negotiation skills can be learned. You may need to develop these skills and practice them with your mom.

4. **Set limits for any abusive or addictive behavior.** Distance is appropriate in cases of abuse, addiction, or whenever your safety is at question. If you state ahead of time that you will leave the room or the house if and when your mom becomes abusive or engages in addiction while you are with her, follow through. The message to your mom is, "I want a relationship with you, but you have to stop the abuse and/or the addiction in order for me to feel safe." It's an important message. You are no longer a helpless child. You can set boundaries and leave when they are violated.

STRATEGIES FOR OVERCOMING FUSION

If you answered yes to the previous questions that helped you clarify whether your relationship with your mom is one of fusion, here are some strategies to help you establish your autonomy while still maintaining a rewarding bond.

1. Don't let yourself be loaded with guilt over unrealistic expectations. There's no time like the present to start asserting yourself. For example, if your mom insists that you are a "bad daughter" if you don't go see Grandma in the nursing home every day, and you know this is unrealistic and unrelated to your feelings for your grandma, tell her you can't promise to go every day but that you still love Grandma. If she gets mad, simply restate your position, calmly and politely. If she pulls away because you've taken that position, let her. Chances are she'll come to her senses. If she doesn't, it's her loss and she's being childish. You don't have to keep operating under unhealthy guilt.

2. Schedule activities with your current family and friends. Don't be available to do everything your mother asks. Have a life away from her; schedule activities with other family and friends. She may not like it, but it's the healthiest choice for you.

3. Establish realistic boundaries. Don't tell your mom every time you take a breath. She doesn't need a play-by-play recitation of your life. Some women get very mad about their mom's intrusiveness, and yet they invite it in by failing to set appropriate boundaries. You can have an intimate connection with her without giving her every detail of your life. For example, if your mom wants to know if your husband is satisfying you sexually, say, "Mom, that is really a private matter between my husband and me. I don't feel comfortable talking to you about it."

4. Stop asking for approval. If you find yourself constantly seeking your mother's approval, stop! You are a grownup who should be able to decide what is right and wrong for yourself. The only One you really need to please is God. His approval matters more than anyone's. If you are keeping His commandments and following His directives—and relating to your mom accordingly—then you don't need the approval of others.

5. Control your emotional impulses. If you have trouble thinking before acting, stop and consider your words and actions before you speak or act. We get in trouble when we impulsively act and say whatever comes into our head. Think about the power of your words, and learn to control your tongue. In the same way that you don't like constant criticism, neither does your mother. Find positive things to say as you work out problems in your relationship.

It's Complicated

It is important to remember that when you take an "I" position with your mom, you'll sometimes get a positive reaction and other times a negative one. That's normal; mothers and daughters do think differently often due to generational and cultural contexts, a topic we discussed earlier.

Understand that all mothers and daughters go back and forth on their feelings about each other. Often after a mom dies, the daughter will tell me she feels a real sense of loss that Mom isn't there to defend her. Yet this was the same daughter who was upset with her mom when she was alive. This speaks to the importance and complication of the mother-daughter bond.

Our task as daughters is to balance our need for intimacy with our need to be autonomous. To do this, we need to continue to develop a better sense of our "I" to lend to the "we." Then we can begin to sort out our needs and her needs and be less impulsive in the way we react to her.

As we develop a better sense of autonomy, we can come to appreciate our differences and learn to communicate more honestly. We don't have to fear that our sense of self will be swallowed up in some unhealthy fusion; we'll recognize when we are allowing that to happen—and stop it.

It's every mother's and daughter's desire to be known by the other. It is also a sign of our maturity when we can think, feel, and behave according to our own beliefs without just reacting to emotional triggers from the other. We are our mother. And yet we aren't. It's a juxtaposition with which we live.

In fact, this juxtaposition is also true with God. As part of humanity, we are called to Him, and we're called to become like Him—to take on His character, to love as He loves, to lose our lives in order to find them.[2] Yet He gives us free will to determine the extent of that intimacy and never forces us to love Him. Through chosen intimacy with God, we discover who we are, we find our spiritual voices, and we declare the glory of God though our lives.

We are God's daughters, fearfully and wonderfully made. Chosen. With God, our perfect Parent, our voices are uninhibited by the past or by problematic relationships, because in Him there is no work or strain. He tells us to come as we are. Accepted. Forgiven. Approved. He wants to know us and for us to know Him. Only then will our voices be strong and sure.

Begin Your Legacy

If you are a mother, you may be thinking, *Did I ever really come to terms with my own autonomy or independence before I became a mother?* As you think back over the years, you may come to the conclusion that you skipped this important step in your own growth and development. Perhaps you were too busy pleasing others, trying to live up to expectations, operating out of guilt, or just too busy to think about your own needs.

The good news is, it's never too late to begin and give this gift to your daughter. Courageously show her the way. If you embark on this journey you will be giving your daughter an important gift—a mother with a developed "I."

According to family therapist Peggy Papp, "The most important thing one woman can do for another is give her a sense of her own possibilities, to expand her awareness of her own potential."[3] The more you find your voice and use it, the more you help your daughter find hers.

Thought Points

1. What similarities do you see in you and your mother? List both positive and negative ones.

2. Looking at the questions in the chapter, how self-defined do you feel? What has helped or blocked your development in this area?

3. Consider how you handle anxiety and tension in your relationship with your mother. Do you tend to be distanced or fused? Most of us operate somewhere on a continuum with these two extremes. What changes could you make to balance autonomy with intimacy?

4. Do you take responsibility for your own decisions, or do you tend to blame the other?

5. Are you just reacting to your mother without thinking through your position? If so, practice slowing down and defining your position clearly to her.

FORGIVENESS: THE HEALING BALM

It was a friday night, and I was looking forward to a real treat: an evening alone. My husband was out of town on business, and both children were at sleepovers. For one full evening, I would do what I wanted to do—read a novel, take a long hot bath with candles and bubbles. I didn't want to plan anything, just let the night unfold. All I knew was that it would involve *quiet.*

It had been an extremely stressful week, and I would have to leave for the airport early the next morning to speak at a conference. First, I needed to pack and take a much-needed break. With anticipation like that of a giddy child, I changed into comfortable clothing. Then I decided to make a quick trip to the grocery store. Since I didn't have to deal with dinner, I bought adult snack food, cheeses and shrimp, and of course, chocolate.

As soon as I arrived home and began to unpack the goodies, the phone rang. It was my daughter, crying and uncertain about her plans. She wanted to come home. The rule in our house is, no matter where you are, if you need to come home, Mom or Dad comes and gets you.

For a brief moment my heart sank, but my disappointment soon faded as I heard her distress on the other end of the line. She needed Mom. I hurriedly put my snacks away and got into the car. The fifteen-mile trip gave me time to grieve my lost night of rest. *Oh well,* I thought, *another time.* (One can always hope!)

After I retrieved my daughter and thanked the people for having her over, we drove back home with lively conversation. She just wanted to be in her own bed tonight and home with Mom. The stress of the past week had affected her, too. We both knew we needed some downtime.

It was getting late. I still had to pack for my early morning flight and make new arrangements to drop Katie off at her friend's house in the morning. This meant I needed to head out an hour earlier than planned so I could make my flight.

"OK, it's going to be an early morning," I told her. "You need to get to bed, and I need to pack."

"But I'm not tired now. Can't we stay up a little longer and watch *Lizzie McGuire?* Please, please."

"OK, let's get PJs on. You can rest in my bed and watch a little. Then up to your room and lights out."

Finally all settled in (it was now 11:00 p.m.), we were ready to call it a night. I still had to pack and be up by 6:30 a.m. Katie returned to her bedroom, and I got busy. Around midnight, I heard her get up and use the bathroom. Then I heard her yell.

"Mom, the toilet's overflowing!"

I ran upstairs, and sure enough, there were two inches of water covering my freshly scrubbed floor. Water was everywhere, and Katie was hauling beach towels from the hall closet to sop up the water. I was impressed with how fast she acted, but the water continued to flow.

Before long, she was crying and I had reached my limit, trying unsuccessfully to stop the water. "Please don't cry. Just tell me what happened." She proceeded to inform me that the four-year-old who had visited our house earlier that day had stuffed toilet paper in the commode. There was so much paper that it soaked up all the water in the bowl. In an effort to clear the clog, Katie had flushed the toilet. At the time, the flush had appeared to be successful. But now it was obvious that the TP had stopped up the line. "It's my fault," Katie cried.

"It's not your fault," I said. "You thought you were helping. And little boys love to stuff anything in holes. It's OK." Water was still pouring everywhere, now with tiny bits of toilet paper floating in it. "I just don't know how to stop it," I said, my volume rising and my tone sharpening.

I was losing it. It was after midnight. There was no one around to help us, and we were both physically exhausted. Katie's crying became louder and more distressed. She was having a meltdown. Water was pouring over the floor in a never-ending flood, and now my voice turned into screaming. "Get the plunger!" I yelled.

"No, call Dad!" Katie yelled back.

Everything in me hated that idea. I didn't want her to think that two females couldn't handle this situation, but Plumbing 101 was not in my PhD program. Honestly, I didn't have a clue why all this water kept pouring out of the toilet bowl.

Reluctantly, I called my husband. He tried to help, but everything he suggested I'd already done. Then he tried to calm me down, but of course that only got me more worked up. I was secretly angry that he wasn't home and I was having to deal with this mess! I knew I was being unreasonable, but I was too upset to think rationally. In frustration, I hung up on him, convinced it was his fault for leaving town!

"Did Dad say what to do?" Katie asked, tears still streaming down her cherub face.

"He had some ideas, but we've already tried them, " I replied with an increasingly testy tone.

My next step was to yell at the water to stop. My frustration was flowing as much as the water. And then I looked over at my little girl's sobbing face. She looked tired and scared, and her mom, a professional therapist, was acting like a raving lunatic. She had just been through a difficult night—wanting to make the sleepover but not feeling ready, up too late, Dad gone, and Mom leaving in the morning. Earlier in the day, she asked me to read her "to-do list" (she is her mother's daughter!) to make sure she had packed everything she needed for the night. At the bottom of the list, scrawled in her handwriting, was "Try not to be scared."

Now she was with her mother, the one she expected to soothe her, and this trusted protector was acting like a madwoman. As we threw every beach towel we had in the house on that soaked floor, I knew I had to get control. I was yelling and crying, basically showing her what not to do when a problem erupts.

Leaving the soaked towels, I moved her to her bedroom. "Katie, let's just sit here a minute. I need to calm down, and so do you. I'm sorry I yelled. I'm out of control. I want to sit here and pray right now." I took a breath, then said, "God, forgive me for panicking and not trusting or turning to You."

Then I turned to face my trembling daughter. "Katie, it is OK to cry, and I shouldn't have scared you by getting so angry. This really isn't your fault. And even if it was—and it's not—it was an accident. It's fixable. We just haven't figured out how to fix it yet. You have been incredibly brave and had the great idea to pick up the carpets and get the beach towels. You are such a thinker. Thank you for doing that and for helping so much. And I shouldn't have yelled at Daddy. That was wrong. I'll have to apologize for that later. He really was trying to help."

Now, I knew what we needed to do. Together we prayed again. I needed to calm down (a recurring theme in my life) and get a plan. "God, we need some help here," I began. "I'm sorry I got so angry. I am calming down now. We know You are here and will help us. Would You please unclog that toilet so we can get to bed? We're in one of those 'times of trouble,' so we are asking for help. OK, God, we are ready."

I kissed her, and she hugged me. Now calm and with new resolve, we were a team. "Let's go tackle that toilet one more time," I told Katie. "This time, the water is going to stop because God is going to knock that clog loose!" As we headed back to the water-soaked bathroom, armed with the plunger, we both started to laugh. We were still giggling as Katie stood by my side and coached. "OK, Mom, get a good plunge. Go deep."

I plunged that plunger and prayed. Then we watched in amazement as something loosened and the water began to flow down the toilet instead of over onto the floor. As we cheered and then thanked God, we finally headed off to bed.

In the morning, when I woke her, Katie smiled. "We did it, and we didn't even need Dad."

"That's because we had our heavenly Father," I answered her. "Don't ever forget that He's always with us. I did forget that for a while last night, but then I remembered. And look how He helped us. You are never alone, Katie. Always remember that God is by your side so you don't have to panic like Mom did. And remember, too, that even when we forget and make a mistake, He forgives us just like you forgave me, and just like Dad will forgive me. Boy, we learned a lot last night!"

"We sure did," she replied. "I'm never flushing a clogged toilet again!"

Mothers aren't perfect. We get stressed, lose our tempers, yell too much, and often regret our actions. If we're honest, we make mistakes and pray they don't send our daughters to psychotherapy one day! We struggle with guilt concerning our imperfections, in part because we believe the myth that mothers are all-caring, all-knowing, and all-nurturing. It's an impossible expectation to meet.

As mothers, we are always teaching by our actions. We need to remember that it's not so much what we say but how we behave that counts. When the bathroom flooded, I started out by unintentionally teaching my daughter to panic in the time of crisis and to yell at those around her. Fortunately, I saw what I was doing and corrected the teaching. Being female, I'm her primary model of how women behave, and with that comes great responsibility. Not condemnation but responsibility. We do the best we can.

If you are willing to acknowledge your faults, your daughter will see you as genuine and real. Then you are in a position to model the correction and free your daughter from her need to be perfect. The message is this: mistakes happen, but we can correct them and grow.

The question for all of us adult daughters to consider is, How do we react to the mistakes, weaknesses, and failures of our mother? Our mother is a woman who sometimes buckles under stress and doesn't always make the right decisions. She blows it. Whether it's a clogged toilet or a serious offense like abuse, our response to our mother's imperfections matters. Our reactions can take us down a road of anger and bitterness, or we can choose a different path, the healing path of forgiveness.

Forgiveness Is Key

If you are a student of the Bible, you know the importance Jesus places on forgiveness. In recent years, even academics have joined the charge to forgive. The personal benefits of forgiveness are now proven. Not only does forgiveness improve your chances for reconciliation, but it is also associated with improved mental and physical health, for example, with lower levels of anxiety and depression, and improved esteem and self-control.

Not everyone shares this high opinion about the importance of forgiveness, however. Susan Battley, clinical associate professor and consulting psychologist at State University of New York at Stony Brook, made this comment about people who have been physically and emotionally battered by their parents: "To say 'You must forgive' is coercive and I think does people a disservice. There are some things that, frankly, are unforgivable. The idea that you'll be free if you take certain steps is demeaning and counterproductive. These people have damaged souls, and some of them may never recover."[1]

Dr. Battley needs to put her words to the test and review the numerous studies that point to forgiveness as a healing balm rather than a disservice. She also needs to understand the truth of the gospel. There is no sin that is unforgivable. Jesus died for all, not some, of our sins. There is also no soul too damaged for the power of the cross to transform. In Christ we are made new. The old has passed away. Nothing is too damaged for God to repair. It's His business. In fact, He seems to do His best work with broken and damaged pieces.

Forgiveness is a spiritual act that releases supernatural power. If you don't have spiritual eyes to see and ears to hear, forgiveness makes no sense. And yet, even those who don't understand the spiritual significance of forgiveness receive its benefits. Forgiveness works; it will move you from that stuck place in your mother-daughter relationship toward healing.

Forgiveness is an act of Christian faith and love, a behavior modeled by Christ. Just as He forgave all our sins and took them to the cross, He tells us to do the same for others. The Creator of our emotional selves knows how we are designed. His words are not empty. They bring life and healing. If you call yourself a follower of the Way, you cannot refuse to forgive. It's that simple.

What Forgiveness Isn't

In talking to mothers and daughters, I have found that they often confuse forgiveness with other things. Forgiveness does not mean that one forgets what happened. Our actions can cause incredible hurt and pain that don't get wiped away simply because we say we are sorry. But forgiveness is an important step in the healing process. Janet's story is a powerful demonstration of this.

For years, Janet was the targeted daughter for her mother's anger and hatred. A violent alcoholic, Janet's mother directed her anger at Janet through repeated beatings and verbal degradation. Early in life, Janet turned to food to be her friend. Unable to soothe herself from the beatings and verbal attacks, food comforted her for the moment. The heavier she became, the more her mom attacked her. She was an embarrassment, her mother said, a "fat pig," a "mistake," and the bane of her mother's existence. Every chance she could, Janet's mother reminded Janet of how much she despised her presence in the home.

As soon as Janet was old enough to leave home, she did. She had little to no contact with her mom. One day, long after she left home and was married, Janet received a phone call from her aunt telling her that her father had died suddenly and her mother was very ill. The aunt wanted Janet to come home and make arrangements for her mom. Both of Janet's sisters had refused.

Little had changed in her mother's life. The alcohol had shut down her liver and she was dying. When her aunt asked her to help, Janet's first response was, "Why would you ask me? You know how much my mom hates me."

But the aunt was desperate. No one would step up to the plate to help, and someone had to move her to a place of care and deal with her husband's will. Janet's impulse was to hang up the phone. The hurt of all those years welled up inside her. She wanted to eat. The thought that first filled her mind was, *Let her suffer. She's getting what she deserved after all the years of beating me.*

But something else inside her knew that her current problems and her overeating had something to do with the resentment and hurt she carried. She decided to make the trip. The thought of seeing her mother for the first time in years created tremendous anxiety, but her fears subsided when she saw the frail, bedridden woman who was dying—only the shell of her mother.

Janet marveled at how much pain this now-emaciated woman had caused her throughout her life. The power of her anger, hate, and addiction had been overwhelming to Janet as a child and teen. *It's not fair,* she thought. *I want to hate her now but she looks so pitiful and frail.*

She left the hospital room, sat in her car, and screamed, "It's not fair! It's not fair! I hate her! Help me, God. I want to hate her, but I'm having trouble."

As she sat in the parking lot of the hospital and dealt with the news that her mom had only days to live, she decided she no longer wanted the burden of offense she had carried all these years. This would be her only chance to make peace. She knew she had to forgive her mom. Yet, little had changed. Her mom was still cantankerous and irritable. And she certainly didn't admit to any wrongdoing over the years.

As Janet entered the hospital room again, she closed the door and whispered into her mom's ear, "I forgive you for all the hurt, beatings, and ugly things you did to me. God will forgive you too if you ask Him. Forgive me for hating you and wishing you dead."

There was no response. Her mom said nothing and turned her

body away from her daughter. A few days later she died, never asking for forgiveness or giving it to Janet.

But as Janet left the hospital, she felt a lifelong burden had lifted. Even though her mother didn't deserve her forgiveness and had never asked for it, Janet knew the significance of what she had done. She needed to be released from a life of guilt, shame, and bitterness. This step of forgiveness was the beginning of her healing. The pain was intense, but Janet was determined to break the generational cycle of hatred and anger. And she knew that hanging on to unforgiveness would only lead to more overeating and numbing of her childhood pain. The work to grieve the many losses would be difficult, but she had taken the first step.

Forgiveness is often a solo action. It is something you choose to do, an act of the will done in obedience to God. Daughters can forgive their mother and not be reconciled. That was the case in Janet's story. She was able to forgive, but reconciliation required the cooperation of her mother, and her mother would not cooperate, even in the face of death.

Although it is the heart of God for reconciliation to occur (see Matthew 5:24), an individual cannot always make this happen. The same is true for mothers. A mother can forgive the daughter, but the daughter may choose not to reconcile with her mother. Reconciliation is interpersonal and requires each to trust.

When you forgive, you are not saying what happened was OK. In Janet's case, it was not OK for her mom to beat and degrade her. It was abusive. Clients often say, "But if I forgive my mother, that means I condoned what she did." This is not true. It only says, I forgive what happened, right or wrong. Janet had no doubt that her mother's beatings and verbal abuse were wrong. Forgiving her mom did not mean she was condoning those behaviors. On the contrary, she forgave horrendous injustices done to her.

Another problem I encounter with forgiveness is the notion that if I forgive someone, I am saying what he or she did wasn't that bad. One has to wonder if that is at the heart of Dr. Battley's statement. Forgiving never minimizes what happened to a person. For example, Janet wasn't saying physical abuse wasn't a big deal. It was a big deal—and it was the root of her compulsive overeating. Forgiveness says that whatever happened was a big deal and that's why I have to let go of the offense. I don't want the repeated offenses to continue to have power over me and become roots of bitterness.

Finally, daughters have asked, "If I forgive my mom, am I not, in a way, pardoning her?" The answer is no. Forgiveness is not so much about what you do for your mother, it's more about releasing you from her offense. The consequences of your mother's actions remain. The same is true when your mother chooses to forgive you. She forgives the offense, but the consequences of your actions play out. In Janet's case, she had no real peace concerning her mother's eternal state. Her mother's refusal to confess and her lack of spiritual commitment had eternal consequences. Janet had to live with this sadness. And Janet also had to accept the fact that her mother refused to reconcile with her.

What Forgiveness Is

I like developmental psychologist and forgiveness researcher Robert Enright's definition of forgiveness: "A willingness to abandon's one right to resentment, negative judgment, and indifferent behavior toward the one who unjustly injured us, while fostering the undeserved qualities of compassion, generosity, and even love towards him or her."[2] As we apply this definition to our mother-daughter relationships, it also helps to remember the words of Mother Teresa: "If we really want to love, we must learn how to forgive." Loving our mother means forgiving her.

Forgiveness is a gift, freely given to us and expected to be given to others. When we choose to forgive our mom, we heal. Typically there is a decrease in anxiety and depression and an increase in esteem and well-being, and a supernatural peace.

You notice I keep using the word *choose*. It's an important word because forgiveness is a choice. Usually it's one you make while allowing your emotions to catch up later. Jesus had to choose to die for us. Remember how He agonized in the garden before His death? "Take this cup from me," He pleaded, knowing the suffering that would soon follow.[3] His prayer would not be answered. Instead, He surrendered His will to His Father's. He chose to suffer unto death. And in those last moments on the cross, His compassion for us cried out, "Father, forgive them; for they know not what they do."[4]

It's an unthinkable picture. Jesus betrayed, rejected, abandoned, teased, abused, cursed, spit upon, mocked, beaten. He experienced every emotion related to abandonment, neglect, and abuse. All of the sins of humanity weighed on Him as He allowed Himself to suffer for our eternal life. He knows firsthand our griefs and sorrows. He chose to take the sins of the world and forgive humanity. Now He tells us to do the same. Can we do any less?

It's Not an Easy Road

The words in Luke 6:37, "Forgive, and you will be forgiven," are not easy to apply. Sometimes forgiveness is only possible because of the transforming power of God. Our human nature wants to retaliate, to watch someone suffer when he or she has hurt us; we hope that person receives justice for the wrongs done to us. Forgiveness is not usually our first response to emotional pain. So we have to work on it: make the choice and trust our emotions will follow.

With our mom, we need an attitude of forgiveness to permeate our relationships. We must stay open to forgiveness. Recall the words of John 20:23, "If you forgive anyone his sins, they are forgiven; if you do not forgive them, they are not forgiven." This is a powerful verse that implies responsibility on our part. We need to forgive and release our mom from the wrongs done to us.

THE FORGIVING PROCESS

So how do we forgive? When you feel you've been wronged by your mom, it disrupts your relationship. Your feelings of love are challenged by the inconsistency of what is happening. Anger usually erupts as the injustice is noticed and allowed to play out. Most of us want an apology when someone treats us unfairly. We may ask for one but we don't always get it. When we don't get an apology or an admission of guilt, we begin to feel and act like a victim—powerless and helpless to make the other person behave correctly.

When that happens with your mom, it is important to value your relationship and try to be empathetic. As an adult, you aren't a victim. You've been wronged, but empathy brings compassion and understanding to the context of the offense. This doesn't excuse her behavior, but at least it gives you a wider lens from which to understand it. Then you can pray for her and ask God to show her the problem.

Empathy also helps us avoid a dangerous split. When a mom-related hurt comes our way, we tend to split our mother into the bad mom versus the good mom. If you can avoid this splitting, it will help. Try to see her as made up of many parts. There are good parts and not-so-good parts. When you are wronged, you are experiencing a not-so-good part of her. No one is all bad all the time.

When you are wronged, there is also a tendency to protect yourself with anger. Anger feels more powerful than hurt; it keeps you from feeling vulnerable. This is when you need to stay open to forgiveness. If you've been deeply hurt, will you be open? You don't have to say yes right away. More often, we have to wrestle with a willingness to even be open to forgive.

Another step in the forgiveness process applies when you feel the offense is too severe or too big to forgive. Unthinkable things happened to you, and either Mom didn't protect you or was the perpetrator. Or perhaps you feel too much has happened since the original hurt occurred, too much time has passed, and you just aren't empowered to forgive. None of that is true. You make the decision to forgive. Granted, serious offenses may take more effort and may require the help of a therapist or minister. But you can forgive any offense because of the power of Christ in you. He wouldn't instruct you to forgive and then not help you do it!

If you find yourself wrestling with forgiveness, make a decision to go forward and determine to do it. Go back to the chapter on developing empathy and follow the guidelines. Decide today that forgiveness is possible and that you will stay open to it. Use chapter 2 as a guide to release anger and offenses, and ask God to help you trust His Word—as you forgive others, you will be forgiven. Forgiveness is an act of obedience to God. You may have to take a step in faith and not act according to your feelings. Then trust that the benefits God promises will happen. You don't have to carry unforgiveness around like a millstone on your neck. Take off the weight of that burden and nail it to the cross. Provision has already been made.

If there are any areas of unforgiveness between you and your mom, bring them up or recall them; try to be empathetic. Remember, you have made mistakes and benefited from forgiveness; now appropriate that same gift to her. Then hold on to that forgiveness no matter how much you start to doubt. Review the scriptures below to reinforce your actions and allow your heart to stay open to forgiveness. These verses can also help renew your mind, even when your "flesh" wants to act otherwise.

Ephesians 1:7: "In him we have redemption through his blood, the forgiveness of sins, in accordance with the riches of God's grace."

Psalm 32:1: "Blessed is he whose transgressions are forgiven, whose sins are covered."

Micah 7:18: "Who is a God like you, who pardons sin and forgives the transgression of the remnant of his inheritance? You do not stay angry forever but delight to show mercy."

Matthew 6:12: "Forgive us our debts, as we also have forgiven our debtors."

Matthew 6:14: "For if you forgive men when they sin against you, your heavenly Father will also forgive you."

Luke 6:37: "Do not judge, and you will not be judged. Do not condemn, and you will not be condemned. Forgive, and you will be forgiven."

Luke 17:4: "If he sins against you seven times in a day, and seven times comes back to you and says, 'I repent,' forgive him."

2 Corinthians 2:10: "If you forgive anyone, I also forgive him. And what I have forgiven—if there was anything to forgive—I have forgiven in the sight of Christ for your sake."

Colossians 3:13: "Bear with each other and forgive whatever grievances you may have against one another. Forgive as the Lord forgave you."

FORGIVE YOURSELF

While some of you are concentrating specifically on forgiving your mother for what she did or didn't do, others of you have trouble forgiving yourself. I've seen this over and over in therapy—adult women who have hurt their mom or disappointed Mom due to making poor life choices. These daughters have apologized but still feel condemned. For some reason, they haven't been able to accept forgiveness.

If you're one of these daughters, it's time to let go of that self-condemnation. It's blocking your mother-daughter intimacy. Sin, once confessed, is gone. The consequences may remain, but you are spiritually clean. If you struggle with unhealthy guilt, pray and ask God to remove the negative thoughts that are keeping you in emotional captivity.

You may also want to use the thought-stopping technique mentioned earlier. Stop the thought that says, *I'm no good. I'm horrible. I'm sinful. I'm guilty. I'm a bad daughter.* Replace it with a renewed thought, and remember Romans 8:1, 4: "Therefore, there is now no condemnation for those who are in Christ Jesus, . . . who do not live according to the sinful nature but according to the spirit." Once you are one of His, you live according to the Spirit. And the Spirit is truth. The truth is that you are forgiven and released from condemnation.

Whatever you did to your mom that keeps you in emotional bondage was something you *did*, not who you *are*. Confess those specifics, be remorseful, grieve the losses that resulted, and then accept your forgiveness.

FORGIVE GOD

One of the blocks to forgiveness can be unforgiveness directed at God. Sometimes we don't even know that we have unforgiveness. For example, when I was thirty and my husband and I decided to have children, nothing happened for seven years. After a miscarriage, my husband and I were diagnosed with undefined infertility. We represented 4 percent of couples who appear to be able to have children but for some unknown reason, don't. This seven-year period in my life was extremely difficult to handle and emotionally exhausting. Many times I struggled with anger at God. How could a loving God not answer my prayer for children? What did I do to deserve this? Was I being punished? Was God unfair? I doubted who He was and His goodness toward me.

There came a point in this long journey when I had to recognize and deal with my anger at God. The root of this anger was doubt. He didn't do what I thought He should do when I thought He needed to! It wasn't until I confessed this doubt that I began to heal emotionally. I also had to believe His Word, that His plans for me were good and that He could make beauty from the ashes of my mourning and loss. The release came when I let go of unforgiveness toward God and then confessed my doubt.

Perhaps you are angry with God for the family in which you were born. Or maybe you are angry because you were abused, neglected, or betrayed by a mother who may have been mentally ill or out of control. Tell God you are angry, but don't remain in a place of unforgiveness. Release it today. He knows what you've experienced. In His sovereignty, He doesn't always intervene to stop mothers from exercising their will and their sinful nature. Bad things happen. Women suffer. Frankly, I don't get it either. I've often wondered why a client was born into a family of sexual abusers and I was not. I don't have answers for the whys. But I do trust God to have the big picture and work all things for our good. We weren't promised a life without trials and suffering, but we are promised His presence, His abiding peace, and His supernatural and unconditional love. I offer you Jesus, a Man acquainted with your grief who bore your sorrows. By His stripes you can be healed.

Forgive the Dead

When mothers die, all the loose ends of the mother-daughter relationship begin to surface. As I mentioned in chapter 2, unresolved anger or other unfinished business often rears its ugly head after death. A wide range of emotions can be felt: anger, guilt, agitation, hate, contempt, relief, deep sorrow, grief, depression. Of course, the best advice I can give is to make peace with your mom *before* she dies. But if it is too late for that, it's not too late to forgive her and heal.

Write down the offenses you have against your mom. Take each one and ask God to forgive you for holding on to it. Release all those offenses to Him. When you have finished, tear up the list. They are gone and done. Choose forgiveness and then work through the consequences of those problems with a therapist or counselor.

Finally, write down a few good memories of your mom. Note what influenced her choices in life. Try to understand where things went wrong and why the two of you never made amends. Then commit to not repeating those patterns in your other relationships.

Mothers and God

If you are reading this and feeling hopeless about making changes with your mom, there are steps you can still take. Here's an exercise that might help you.

On a piece of paper, make two columns. Label one column MOTHER and the other GOD. Look up scriptures about the character of God and His relationship to us. For example, Isaiah 43:4 says God considers us precious and honored. So, in the GOD column, write "sees me as cherished and honored." Under the MOTHER column write down your perception of whether or not that is also true with your mother, that is, whether your mother also cherishes and honors you.

Using another example, Psalm 9:10 tells us that God is trustworthy. Under GOD, write "trustworthy." Then, under MOTHER, write whether you feel that is true or not. An example is shown below:

GOD	MOTHER
Sees me as cherished and honored	No
Trustworthy	She has betrayed my trust several times

After you've developed a long list, begin to pray over those areas in which you feel your mother doesn't measure up. Ask God to forgive you of any anger or bitterness concerning her perceived failures. Then ask God to give you a personal revelation of His love and truth related to each of those attributes. Try to think of instances in which God's unconditional love and acceptance have been shown to you. Then thank Him for making a way for you to feel loved and accepted. Ask Him to somehow help you show His love to your mother. Remember, God gave His love to us in the form of His Son—His very life—so we could be saved. We didn't deserve it, but He gave it anyway.

You may feel your mother doesn't deserve your love, but give it anyway. You will be blessed by this, and God will honor you. It's not about what is fair; it's about what is right and loving to do. Be the bigger person. Take the first step in the relationship without expecting anything in return.

You are already loved and accepted by the One who created you. If you struggle with feelings of rejection related to your mother, try to work it out with her. If that's not possible, then turn to God and find what you need in Him. Give Him the lies that have influenced your thinking because of the rejection. Pray and ask God to reveal Himself and the truth.

Quite a revelation occurs when we experience the unconditional love and acceptance of God. While this revelation doesn't remove our feelings of loss, God's love is perfect and is enough to sustain you in life. Intimacy with Him will correct family loss. How? As you learn to love God with all your heart, soul, and mind, He will pour His love into you, making you more forgiving and compassionate to those who have hurt you. It's a supernatural transformation that occurs, one that's hard to explain in the natural.

Making the choice to forgive your mother is a decision you'll never regret. But those who choose not to forgive often do feel regret. I promise, you won't be disappointed in the results. Forgiveness brings healing and blessing.

A Word on Judgment

Forgiveness and judgment are such close bedfellows that I often get them mixed up. When someone hurts me or treats me unfairly, I am quick to forgive. But where I used to fall short was releasing that person to the judgment of God. I wanted him or her to suffer the consequences of the injustice committed against me. Secretly I hoped the person would fail or get his or her "just deserts." I'm being honest here, and it isn't pretty. Oh, I never proclaimed judgment on those who hurt me, at least not out loud. But I knew what was in my heart, and it bothered me. I knew the scriptures:

Psalm 75:7: "But it is God who judges: He brings one down, he exalts another."

Matthew 7:1: "Do not judge, or you too will be judged."

Luke 6:37: "Do not judge, and you will not be judged. Do not condemn, and you will not be condemned. Forgive, and you will be forgiven."

Several years ago, God put me to the test. I had been lied to and betrayed by a friend. She never admitted her deception and appeared to prosper after all that happened. One day, when I was sitting at lunch with one of my spiritual mentors who knew about the problem, she asked me how I was doing with forgiving this person. I told her I had long ago forgiven the offense. Then she asked me a question that pierced my heart: "How are you doing when it comes to judging her?"

"What? What do you mean?" I asked innocently.

"You know what I mean," my friend replied. "Are you secretly hoping something bad will happen to her? Are you holding her in judgment? You seemed to be so concerned about the fact that she appears to be doing well."

Ouch! This was definitely a touchy question. I had to admit I was judging her.

My friend suggested I devote time in prayer to this and let God do the judging. As I prayed, I realized I was holding on to judgment. In my heart, I was a little happy when I heard that her life had hit a snag. And I wasn't able to pray a blessing on her. Oh, I said the words, but my heart wasn't in it. What released me was being reminded of my own sin. God's grace and mercy to me were incredible. How could I accept His grace and then not give it to others?

I am no better than anyone else. My sinful nature rears its ugly head far too often, and I am back on my knees. God's grace is where we live daily. He is the judge, not us. My husband often reminds me that I am not the Holy Spirit. We can all be thankful for that! Don't take on the job. God always has it and He isn't asking for helpers.

Grace under Fire

Grace counters judgment. Thank God for His amazing grace. Walk in that grace and then appropriate it to your mom and others. Whenever I struggle to be gracious to anyone, I think about a story from Max Lucado's book *In the Grip of Grace*. I've used this story many times to illustrate the grace of God.

Lucado begins his chapter on godless judgment by asking a haunting question, "You know what disturbs me most about Jeffrey Dahmer?" (Dahmer was the serial killer who cut up his multiple victims and ate their body parts.) Lucado repeatedly asks this question throughout the chapter after he describes horrendous and incomprehensible things about this man. By the time Lucado revisits this question for the last time, you want judgment for this killer.

But here's the kicker. According to Lucado, Dahmer was converted to Christ before he died; he repented for all he did. He was forgiven, and that troubled Lucado (and the rest of us reading this story). We had him condemned, undeserving of any human kindness. JUDGMENT! That's what we wanted. But Dahmer repented, and Lucado wrote what all of us are thinking: "Grace is for average sinners like me, not deviants like [Dahmer]."[5]

The message is clear; we can't point our finger at others because when we do, we condemn ourselves. We can convict Dahmer of his unspeakable crimes, and he will pay the penalty for murder, and we can be repulsed by his unnatural actions. But, as Lucado points out, he is not beyond the grace of God.

Think about the grace of God when it comes to your mother-daughter relationship. If there is grace for serial killers, there is grace for the two of you. It's time to lay aside judgment and stop looking for repayment. While we all enjoy living in a just society, we have a higher calling when it comes to interpersonal justice. When we appropriate God's grace, the enemy of our souls has little room to play. Because of this, he can't keep us bound. Grace is needed for mother-daughter relationships.

We'll talk more about grace in the final section of this book, but for now I will conclude this chapter with the words of the apostle Paul. It's straight talk when it comes to holding our mom in judgment:

> *You, therefore, have no excuse, you who pass judgment on someone else, for at whatever point you judge the other, you are condemning yourself, because you who pass judgment do the same things. Now we know that God's judgment against those who do such things is based on truth. So when you, a mere man, pass judgment on them and yet do the same things, do you think you will escape God's judgment? Or do you show contempt for the riches of his kindness, tolerance and patience, not realizing that God's kindness leads you toward repentance.* (Romans 2:1–4)

THOUGHT POINTS

1. Are you holding on to unforgiveness in your relationship with your mother? If so, are you ready to make peace over that issue?

2. What is your understanding of forgiveness? Have you been unwilling to forgive because you thought it meant condoning, minimizing, or pardoning the behavior?

3. Have you forgiven your mother but not reconciled a relationship problem?

4. Take an existing offense and ask to be forgiven—or be proactive in forgiving your mother for an offense.

5. Consider your ability to forgive yourself and/or God. Are you stuck in these two areas? If so, talk about why.

6. Are you holding your mom in judgment? If so, appropriate God's grace and release that judgment.

IO

THE GOOD-ENOUGH DAUGHTER:
LETTING GO OF GUILT AND SHAME

I CONSIDER MYSELF a fairly healthy person, but I've spent way too much of my life feeling as if I could be or do better. It's a problem that plagues most women. One mistake, one flaw, one bad relationship—it doesn't take much to knock us down. Then guilt sneaks in and attacks us.

As daughters, we can feel guilty about anything, all things, irrational things. We have guilt for yelling at our mother too much, for not spending enough time with her, for not calling her enough, for asking her to stop repeating the same story, for harboring feelings of anger, for wishing she would stop telling us what to do, for . . . well, go ahead and name your guilt; this list could go on forever. And what we choose to feel guilty over isn't always big traumatic things. Small things can trip us up.

Take Jenna's recent dilemma concerning how often and when to call her mom. "If I don't call her, she'll think I don't care. If I do call, maybe that means I'm overly dependent. If I don't call, she may feel slighted, like I don't have time for her. And also if I don't call, I won't stay connected.

"How often do I call? Every day seems to be too much. Once a week isn't enough, considering her age and distance. When do we talk? With two small kids, I'm constantly on the run, sitting by the piano making sure the lesson is practiced correctly, monitoring homework, cooking meals, cleaning, doing my own writing and work. It's enough to make me crazy!"

Got Guilt?

Guilt has power over us because we have our own myths about being perfect daughters. When we slip up (as we all do), we have this need to hang on to guilt and beat ourselves over the head with it. It's not that we want to do this, but it feels familiar, like an old nagging friend. So we keep doing it. Well, it's time to drop that unhealthy guilt and move on with life. In this chapter, I'll show you some strategies for doing that.

Courtney's story is a good place to begin. She decided she was ready for a change. The only daughter in a family of five, Courtney was married with three teenaged children. After Courtney's father died, Courtney's mother moved into Courtney's house. For years, this arrangement worked smoothly. But suddenly, her mom's health began to decline. At night, Courtney often heard her mother open the back door and wander into the yard. During the day, Mom turned on the gas stove and left it on when no one was home. The diagnosis was made: Mom had Alzheimer's and was deteriorating fast.

Courtney tried to manage Mom at home, but there were times she had to leave her alone there. One day while she was out, Mom slipped and broke her hip. The hospital social worker assessed her mom's condition and strongly recommended it was time for a nursing home. Even though Courtney knew the social worker was right, she couldn't place her mom in a nursing home.

Back home again with Mom, Courtney was determined to make this work. All she thought about was how well Mom had taken care of her all her life. And in these past few years, her mom had been a godsend in helping Courtney with her children. If she put Mom in a home, it felt like she was deserting her. She couldn't do it.

Mom's condition was rapidly worsening. She was so disoriented and forgetful that her actions were becoming dangerous. Courtney knew she could no longer manage her physically, and reluctantly she agreed to place her in a nursing facility.

Painstakingly, she looked for a nursing home for Alzheimer's patients and did all the groundwork necessary to make sure the placement was a good one. But as she drove away from her mom's beautiful new surroundings, all she could do was cry. Her mom didn't even recognize her anymore, but Courtney knew Mom, and the guilt was killing her.

For weeks, Courtney cried. It didn't matter when the staff gave her good reports or when she noticed the dignified treatment they provided her mom. She felt like a traitor. She had abandoned the woman who gave her life, who mended her socks, who scrimped and saved to put her through college.

As she cried and sought comfort, she realized she was not alone. Many of her friends were facing similar situations or had already been down her long and difficult road. There were no easy answers or decisions. But she had to rid herself of the guilt that was physically depleting her.

Guilt, even though it is irrational at times, can have a powerful hold over us. We can feel guilty for things we do and for things we don't do. We can feel guilty for others, guilty for no reason, guilty for even being alive! There doesn't have to be a legitimate reason for guilt to exist. It just does. But unhealthy guilt, if allowed to plague us, can paralyze us emotionally.

Guilty As Charged

Perhaps you are thinking, *Yes, but she doesn't know the things I've done. I'm not a "good girl" like Courtney. My life is a mess because of my decisions.* Then you may relate to Debbie's story.

Debbie sat motionless, deep in thought. The question her therapist asked was one she didn't want to think about. It was too sobering. "If you were standing by your mom's grave right now, what would you want to say?" Flooded with emotion, words wouldn't come.

The emotional pain of the past ten years felt fresh. Rebellious and insolent as an adolescent, Debbie spent her days escaping life through alcohol and drugs. Pregnant at nineteen, she had an abortion and ran away from home. Her life was a mess. Now sober and clean, she was being pushed by the therapist to reconnect with her mom. "Debbie, remember, it was you who left and ran away."

But this question, this awful question, only brought tremendous guilt. What a disappointment she must be to her mother! She stared into space, and the therapist asked again, "If you were standing by your mother's grave . . ."

Debbie's eyes welled up with tears. What would she say? What could she say? She screwed up her courage. Somehow, "Sorry, Mom" didn't seem to cut it. The guilt overwhelmed her again.

But the therapist kept pressing. "Debbie, you can go home again."

Oh, if only that were true, she thought. She wanted to believe it, but something in her head kept saying, *No, you can't. Too much has happened.* As she fought back the tears, she tried to refocus on the question. There was so much to say. She wanted to tell her mom how miserable she was in high school, how much she hated being teased for being shy. She wanted to explain how desperate she was for a boyfriend, how she longed to fit in and how drugs seemed to loosen her up and make her feel less anxious. Maybe if her mother knew she was high on drugs the night she conceived and that she was terrified of having a baby with brain damage, she would understand the fear that drove her to desperation. There was so much to talk about, but she was too ashamed to approach her mother.

"Think about the question, Debbie," the therapist prompted. "If you were standing over her grave, would you regret never trying to reconnect? Would you wish you had said certain things?"

Debbie knew the answers.

The therapist suggested she write down her thoughts in a letter she wouldn't send. She was instructed not to edit her thoughts but to write from her heart with no constraints. Guilt aside, what would she want to say?

Across the page, she immediately scribbled, "I'm sorry I wasn't a good-enough daughter, a daughter who didn't disappoint, a daughter who made good choices and listened to her parents, a daughter who used the opportunities provided, a daughter who respected her body. I never felt good enough to be what I thought you wanted me to be. How did this happen? I think we wanted the same things, but somehow I didn't get on the right path.

As the therapist carefully read the words, it was apparent that guilt and shame were paralyzing Debbie. These feelings were preventing her from contacting her mother. "Look, Debbie, you can't go back and make up lost time or change what happened in the past. But if you've confessed your faults, made a change, and are working hard to renew your thinking and change your behavior, guilt serves no purpose except to immobilize you. Accept your mistakes as such— mistakes. Give up the belief that you should have made the right choices. You didn't, and you were blinded by your hurt and pain. Stop using guilt to further punish yourself for wrongdoings. It's time to release it and connect with your mother. What's the worst thing that could happen?"

"She might refuse to see me or even refuse to speak to me."

"OK, if that happens are you any worse off than now?"

"No, not really. I mean, we don't speak or see each other now."

"Then you've got nothing to lose and everything to gain. Frankly, this letter sounds like your life is over. You are twenty-nine years old. Your mom is still living and has made efforts to contact you. What about the Debbie who has survived the past ten years and has made significant changes? What about the future? What about your life from here on out?" she asked.

"But I also sense that it's more than guilt that's stopping you. There is shame regarding your past. Not only do you keep telling me how many mistakes you've made, but you seem to be saying you are a mistake. We have to address this guilt and shame you carry," she told Debbie.

Weeks later, as Debbie sat at home contemplating her next move, she remembered a picture she had seen in church as a child. In the back of the sanctuary, high on the wall, was a magnificent picture of Jesus. His eyes were piercing, as if they saw right through her. But what she remembered most was His wide open arms. It was as if He wanted to embrace her. Drawn to that picture, she would stare at it, enthralled.

One Sunday, standing in front of the picture, she had asked her mom, "Mom, I think Jesus is reaching out to me, like He wants to hug me or something. But how can He do that?" The memory was vivid. Her mom had reached down, opened her arms, and given her a huge hug. "Debbie, that's why He gave you a mom. So she could hug you until He gets His turn in heaven."

More tears began to flow. Could she go home again? Would her mother's arms be open? Would she hug her and welcome her back? That would feel so good! She missed her mom so much. But a nagging thought kept reentering her brain: after everything that had happened, why would her mother want to see her?

One day, walking around town, she wandered into a church. A women's group was meeting. Debbie wasn't big on organized religion, but a tall, striking woman was telling a story that sounded vaguely familiar. She took a seat in the back of the room and listened. This is the story the woman told:

Once there was a mother who had two daughters. The younger daughter was restless and wanted to see the world and experience all it had to offer. The older daughter was content to stay home and learn from her mother. She never gave her mom a problem. But the younger daughter kept pushing to leave home and go to the city. She was sure that's where she would find excitement and adventure.

Finally, after months of pressuring her mom, the younger daughter's wish to leave home was granted. She could use a sum of money saved for her college education. The daughter packed her bags and left for the big city. Her intention was to experience everything the city had to offer.

For months she partied, met new people, and played around until the money was finally gone. Then, when she was broke, her new friends stopped calling and getting together. Lonely and depressed, with no place to go and no one to talk to, she decided to go home again. "I'm going back to my mother. I'll cook, clean, do whatever she wants me to do. I'll tell her how wrong I was and that I don't deserve to be her daughter." It was settled. She would return to her mother.

When she was still a long way off, her mother saw her coming. The daughter's heart pounded as her mother ran out to greet her. To her complete surprise, her mother embraced and kissed her. "Mother, I've squandered what you gave me. I acted impetuously and have nothing to show for all my time away. I've terribly mismanaged my life. The things I did would greatly disappoint you. I don't deserve to be called your daughter."

But the mother wasn't listening. Instead, she called the family and told them to throw a party. Aunt Sally was to make the daughter a new outfit. Aunt Renee would do her nails. Cousin Ann would loan her all her good jewelry. Grandma would set the table with the finest crystal and china. "We are going to have a wonderful time," the mother said. "My daughter is here. She was given up for dead but is alive. We thought she was lost but is now found. So let the party begin!"

During this incredible reunion, the older sister was hard at work at her office, presenting her new business plan to corporate management. After finishing her presentation, she drove home and heard singing and dancing inside the house. Surprised by all the commotion, she called over a neighbor to ask what was going on. The neighbor squealed with delight, "Oh, your sister—you know the one we all gave up for dead—actually came home. She's in the house right now! Your mom is so thrilled, she's throwing a huge party."

Infuriated, the older sister refused to go inside. "I'm not going in to celebrate such irresponsibility. How can my mother be doing this? Is she crazy?" Her mother came out and tried to talk to her, but the angry daughter wouldn't listen. She yelled, "Look how long I've been responsible and have helped you. I have been the good and dutiful daughter. Have you ever thrown a party for me? My sister returns from her wasted state, having squandered her future, and you throw a party? I'm sorry, but I don't get this."

"Daughter!" the mom exclaimed. "You don't understand. You are with me all the time. Everything I have is yours, but now we have a reason to celebrate. This sister of yours we thought to be dead is alive! We had given up, thinking she was lost, but she has been found."[1]

Debbie knew the story. The storyteller had changed the genders, but she recognized it from the Bible. It was Jesus's parable of the Prodigal Son, as recorded in Luke. The parable's message pierced her heart, reminding her that God is concerned about lost people, values each one of us, and wants us to return to Him. It doesn't matter how far we've strayed from our beliefs and principles, God accepts us with open arms.

Debbie knew her mother prayed for her every day and that she had tried several times to call Debbie. She remembered the compassion of her mother's heart and understood the deep grief she had caused by leaving. Would her mom react like the mother in the parable? Would she welcome Debbie with open arms? It was time to find out. She was going home.

The journey home would not be easy. How would she begin? Should she call or just show up on her doorstep? Calling would be best. That way she could gauge her mom's response. OK, just pick up the phone and do it. But she couldn't. Overwhelmed again with the weight of her past, she agonized for days as to what to say. How do you begin a conversation that ended more than ten years ago? What do you say?

The anxiety drove her back to the therapist's office. "OK, I'm going to try contacting my mom, but I haven't a clue where to start. I need some help here."

The therapist suggested they practice a few conversations. The therapist would role-play Debbie's mom, pretending to react several different ways so Debbie could think through what she would say in different scenarios.

First the therapist practiced being the rejecting mom, then the angry mom, the grieved mom, the stunned mom, and finally the happy mom. Trying to anticipate the mother's possible reactions gave Debbie the confidence she needed to make the call. "The worst thing that could happen to me is that she could hang up or tell me to drop dead. I don't think she'll do either, but if she does, I'm emotionally prepared for it now," she said. "I could be hurt by this, but I've got to try. I don't want to live the rest of my life estranged from my mom because of my bad decisions early on in life. I want her to see the changes I've made, my repentant heart, and my efforts to start over. Most of all, I want to grieve with her over the loss of her grandchild. It's a grief I have carried alone."

Night after night Debbie sat by the phone, praying and trying to muster the courage to call. "You can do this," she would tell herself. "God, help me do this. Prepare her heart to receive me." Finally she punched the numbers on the phone. Her heart began to race, her palms became sweaty, and she felt like she might faint. "Hello," she heard on the other end of the line. That voice, still sweet and loving, was too much. Debbie panicked and quickly hung up the phone.

"God, help me!" she prayed. "I don't want to be rejected again."

Slowly she redialed. This time when she heard her mom's voice, she managed to say, "Mom, it's me, Debbie."

Silence.

Oh no, she thought, *she's not going to speak to me.*

But through tears, she finally heard her mom's voice ask, "Debbie, is it really you?"

"Yes, Mom, it is," she said. "I need to talk to you. I want to make things right between us."

"Debbie, I'm so glad you're safe. You don't know how many nights I've prayed for this call. Please come home. We can talk. I've made mistakes too."

As the two made plans to meet, Debbie was so relieved. The long-anticipated rejection didn't happen. Instead, there was rejoicing. Someone lost was about to find her way home. And while her life was still unsettled, Debbie knew she could proceed. Now she had broken the ice, but the next step would be even more difficult. She would have to face her mother again. The last time they saw each other, Debbie was highly rebellious and said things she now regretted.

Back to the therapist's office. "We need more practice for my face-to-face time with Mom," she said. "Where do I start? I still feel so ashamed of what I've done. And I'm having dreams of my baby dead in my mother's arms. Actually, they are nightmares. I wake up terrified and breathing heavily."

"We'll work on that, Debbie. But first I have to tell you how impressed I am with the step you took," the therapist said. "You found the courage to call. That's huge. Now let's deal with the shame you feel and then the nightmare.

"Whenever you talk about your mother, you mention how bad you are. Shame seems to be your constant companion. What's your first memory of that shame feeling?" Debbie thought for a moment and then recalled a boy in junior high who had teased her about her body. Debbie entered puberty early and was quite developed by the fifth grade. A boy in her class often made crass remarks about the size of her breasts. Already feeling self-conscious about her development, Debbie felt ashamed when he made sexual remarks to her. She didn't know what to say or do and never told anyone about it. Somehow she felt it was her fault and she should have been able to stop him.

One day, the boy approached her and slammed her against the wall of her locker, calling her a tease. Shame overwhelmed her as she also heard another boy make a remark about her body. She retreated and became increasingly shy. If she could fade into the background, maybe the teasing would stop. As the memory was explored, the shame of that period of her life felt real and present.

As she allowed herself to feel that emotional pain, she walked through the healing of that memory with the therapist. At one point, all she could do was sob uncontrollably. The therapist led her in prayer and asked Jesus to reveal His truth to her concerning the lie she believed about her "badness" that had led to this feeling of shame. In a still, small voice, she felt God speak to her, telling her that her body was wonderfully made and that He was never ashamed of His creation.

Then there was peace. The shame of all those years seemed to disappear. For the first time, she was able to know in her heart that she had no role in this shame.

Back to the memories. She had given in to a sexual relationship, hoping a man would love her. But he left her as soon as she realized she was pregnant. There she was in the abortion clinic, having medicated herself with painkillers. Confused and scared, she consented to the abortion, feeling sure her mother would hate her for being sexually active.

Next her memory took her to the aftermath of the abortion. She remembered being wheeled past a woman who was sobbing. That sound pierced her heart as she lay on a table, the abortion just completed, the sound of despair filling the room. *Someone comfort that woman!* Debbie silently screamed. *Make her stop!* But the woman continued. And her crying became louder and louder.

"Debbie, what are you thinking right now?" the therapist asked.

"That woman needs her mother. She needs someone to comfort her. I need my mother. But I am all alone. I feel so alone." At that moment in the memory, Debbie began to sob. The emotion was gut-wrenching, and it seemed that she cried for hours.

"I'm scared that I'll be all alone," she whispered through her tears.

Again the therapist prayed and asked the Lord to speak to her. As He reassured Debbie that He would never leave her or forsake her and that nothing could separate her from His love, Debbie could feel His love. Healing was on its way.

But then it hit her: the life lost, the baby she would never hold. The grief welled up inside. The therapist encouraged her to face this pain, to allow the grief to surface. She had experienced a tremendous loss and needed to grieve. A dam of emotion burst as Debbie sat on the big stuffed chair in the therapist's office and cried for the lost child.

"I keep thinking that what I did was unforgivable," she said, "that if my mother finds out, she will hate me and never want to see me again."

"Debbie, you know that's not true," the therapist said. "When you ask for forgiveness, God is always ready to give it. He wants you to live in His grace. Let's go to Him, and you ask Him to speak this truth to you now."

"I see Jesus standing in front of me," Debbie said. "Actually, it's that picture of Him from the church when I was a child. But in my spirit, I feel He's reminding me of His open arms, that He wants to embrace and love me. And that He has my baby in His arms and wants to comfort me."

"Then let Him," the therapist softly replied.

Something significant lifted from Debbie as she worked through these critical issues. While she didn't justify her bad choices of drugs and sex, she now understood the root causes of her attempts to numb herself from emotional pain. And she learned that she could face this pain and not die. She realized that she had been deceived into thinking she was bad and didn't deserve God's love or her mother's.

After several sessions of working on this issue, Debbie was ready to meet her mom. And though most stories don't have storybook endings, this one came close. You see, Debbie's mom was a woman of prayer. For years, she had prayed and waited for her daughter to come home. She had long ago forgiven her and strongly desired to be reconciled. She prayed that Debbie's heart would stay soft and open to a mother's love.

Debbie was anxious as she prepared for her face-to-face meeting with her mother. But when she saw her, the past—and the anxiety—seemed to melt away. She was back in her mother's arms. Most of the first meeting centered on asking forgiveness, on making things right, on each acknowledging her part of the distancing. And though Debbie's road to sobriety would still be difficult, she now had a praying mother to cheer her along. And together they grieved the child that would never be with them.

It was exhausting work but well worth the effort. Debbie's healing is possible for others. Her story reminds us that there is always hope for reconciliation. Even if Debbie's mother had refused to see her, Debbie knew she had to try. It was the willingness of her heart, the humility of her sin, a yearning to have her mother's love a part of her life again, that allowed her to go home.

Crossing the Bridge over Troubled Waters

Perhaps you feel like Debbie, lost and filled with guilt and shame. You want to reconnect with your mom, but your choices and actions have created a gulf between the two of you. This gulf feels big and difficult to traverse. If you want to find your way back home again, turn in that homeward direction.

Guilt is a natural reaction when you violate your principles and beliefs. Your conscience should signal that something is wrong. Guilt says, "I made a mistake." But hanging on to the guilt once you've acknowledged wrongdoing is unhealthy. Some women hang on to guilt because it is much easier to blame themselves than to deal with the uncertainty and ambiguity of relationships. Others feel guilty because they want to punish themselves.

The natural consequences of your actions will play out, but there is no need to heap guilt on a forgiven past. True remorse and repentance bring change. Once you have confessed your wrongdoing, you must learn to accept the forgiveness that has been given you.

In Debbie's case, she needed to use her guilt to motivate her to make things right with her mom. It was good for her to feel remorse. The problem was that her remorse took on a life of its own and converted into unhealthy and excessive guilt. And it was additionally complicated with intense feelings of shame. Shame comes when you've done something improper or wrong but internalize "badness" because of it. Shame says, "I am a mistake," not "I made a mistake."

Debbie felt flawed, no good, and inadequate because of her experiences. The truth was that she had made poor choices, but she, as a person, was redeemable and not "bad." Her thoughts told her differently, however, and prevented her from reconnecting with her mom.

Shame often develops when daughters have been given messages of being bad, weak, or unloved. Parents, teachers, friends, and boyfriends can humiliate, belittle, and/or criticize a child rather than deal with her inappropriate behavior. When you confuse mistakes or wrongdoing with being "bad," shame results.

Daughters also compare themselves to others and often feel they don't measure up in some area of their lives. We believe we could be more respectful, loving, compassionate, empathetic, less angry, or whatever to correct our perceived fault. The truth is that we aren't perfect. We unconsciously repeat dysfunctional patterns. We respond in needy ways. We carry unrealistic expectations and look to others to make up for the hurts we face. We act out and push people away.

Perhaps we are afraid to love because we've experienced trauma and loss that somehow led to feelings of shame, for example, sexual abuse, humiliation by an alcoholic mother, or having a critical dad who made fun of our weight or body. Whatever the cause, shame is not a welcomed companion. It haunts us and keeps us feeling "not good enough."

As a therapist, I am aware that not all mothers want to repair the tensions and problems with their daughters. There are mothers who would scoff at Debbie and tell her to drop dead. These mothers are so lost in their own emotional pain and pathology that they can't or won't stay connected. They create avenues for guilt and shame, having been generational recipients of both themselves.

If that is your situation, your mother will not be your co-companion toward emotional freedom. You will have to bypass her pathology and find release in the experience and acceptance of God's grace. Whether or not we can work with our mother, the ultimate path of healing is found in God. Because He has forgiven us and we live in grace, not under the Law, we can be free from all that keeps us emotionally bound.

We are created to feel deeply, to mourn, and to grieve losses associated with sin and mistakes. God responds to our grief. Isaiah 61:3 says He will "provide for those who grieve in Zion—to bestow on them a crown of beauty instead of ashes, the oil of gladness instead of mourning, and a garment of praise instead of a spirit of despair. They will be called oaks of righteousness, a planting of the LORD for the display of his splendor."

When you acknowledge your mistakes and your responsibility, you can't hang on to condemnation. If you do, you fail to realize the power of the blood covenant that covers past sins. Yes, you know Jesus died on the cross to take your sin, but for some reason, you can't get past your mistakes; instead you walk around carrying tremendous guilt and shame. He died so you could give Him these sins and burdens. Hand them over, and walk with your head held high.

DAUGHTER, WHERE ARE YOUR ACCUSERS?

She was caught in the act. It was true that she had committed adultery, and now everyone knew it. Standing before her judges, she knew the law. Adultery was punishable by stoning to death. But Jesus saw deep into the hearts of her accusers.

"Throw your stone," He told those gathered to carry out the sentence. "But only throw it if you can say you have no sin." At that moment, you could have probably heard a pin drop. Who could live up to such a claim? One by one, the crowd of accusers dispersed. Jesus had gotten to the heart of the matter: All have sinned and come short of His glory.

The woman stood alone. She was probably stunned and amazed by this man of intense power and love. When He stood up to address her, she must have wondered, *What now will He say? He certainly isn't conventional. The fact that He's even speaking to me is remarkable.*

His next words brought revelation: "Woman, where are your accusers? Does anyone condemn you?"

"No one," she responded.

"Then neither do I. Go and sin no more."

And that was that. She wasn't going to die, even though she deserved to under the law. What kind of Man was this who offered grace instead of condemnation?[2]

Jesus does not accuse you to the Father. He told us so in John 5:45: "Do not think that I shall accuse you to the Father; there is one who accuses you—Moses, in whom you trust" (NKJV). What He meant was that we can never measure up to the Law of Moses. All of us sin and fall short of living a perfect life.

When Jesus came, He took our failings to the cross and became the ultimate sacrifice. Consequently, His blood covers our failings, so we now live under grace, not law. Therefore, when we make mistakes, we are no longer condemned by the old Law but justified through Christ. It is *just as if* we never sinned. We need to understand this.

The accuser is the devil (see Revelation 12:10). He is the one telling us we are no good and unworthy of the blood of Jesus. He continues to throw lies at us, penetrating our thinking until we believe that we deserve to be judged.

We have to fight the accuser by resisting him. He has been thrown down and is under our feet. When Jesus says we are not accused, the Holy Spirit reminds us of His Word so we can stand in truth and resist the lie.

This doesn't mean we go on sinning. Sin leads to death. Remember, Jesus told the woman to stop her sin. So when we sin and then repent, we must walk in the grace Jesus offers. Stop listening to that voice of accusation. It wants you to remain stuck in guilt and shame. In contrast, Jesus wants you to be free.

Whatever your story, let go of guilt and shame. If possible, reconcile with your mother. At least give it a try and see what happens. Don't miss out on a possible relationship simply because you think you've gone too far away or done too much. Like the story of the prodigal daughter, you can't go too far for most moms. Come back home.

Letting Go

To grow up means you let go of unrealistic childhood dreams and learn to accept life on the terms you encounter. Our mother, we learn, is imperfect. Later, we realize the same is true about us. If we don't learn to grieve our losses, we will find ourselves repeating them. The work outlined in this chapter can be summed up with this advice: *Act like a grownup, not a bad little girl. Lose the guilt and shame that keep you in emotional bondage.*

Healthy adults realize that dreams don't always come true, that magical endings only happen in the movies, and that life has much more reality than any television show could ever portray. We are not living our mother's dream. God has given us our own. And for that reason, we must unblock whatever prevents us from becoming who we were intended to be. If your block is guilt and/or shame, then it's time to be empowered by God's love and put the past in the past. Have the courage to approach your mother and deal with any emotional pain you may have caused.

CONFESSION, NOT OBSESSION, IS GOOD FOR THE SOUL

If you are a daughter who feels she has wronged her mother or let her down, face up to your mistakes. Admit what you believe you did that contributed to problems. Identify the problem. In order to do this, you have to be willing to assess your behavior and be humble.

Maybe you're saying, "Well, she hurt me too, so why isn't she asking for forgiveness?" or "Why should I try to make peace? She's the mother!" or "Why should I be the one to call or do anything?" The answer to these questions is always the same: "Because you are a grownup and responsible to God for your behavior, not hers."

So take the first step and ask yourself if you are living up to the standards and moral code in which you believe. If you've wronged your mother, say you are sorry. Worry less about what she is doing and more about the steps you need to take. Admitting wrong is a powerful relationship jolt. It often frees the other person to make a move.

Once you've admitted your mistakes, give her time. She may admit making mistakes too. If she doesn't, forgive her anyway and then ask what the two of you can do to rebuild the relationship. In Debbie's case, her mother wanted to reconnect. But because of Debbie's past behavior (stealing, lying, manipulating), Mom needed to experience her daughter as trustworthy, something that would take time. She was willing, however, to give Debbie another chance.

Debbie's mom also admitted to not dealing well with Debbie's pregnancy. The drug and alcohol involvement really complicated the situation. So she agreed to attend Alanon, a program for family members of an addicted person, in order to learn how to better respond to her now clean and sober daughter. The two women would also work together in therapy to reconstruct their mother-daughter relationship.

If you've let your mother down because of past mistakes, take the steps outlined here to rebuild trust and improve your relationship. Identify those things that block your intimacy, and come up with a plan. You may need to see a therapist or counselor to help you through this process.

The second step is to weigh the amount of responsibility you feel about your guilt. Are you taking all the blame? If your problems were solely caused by you, fine. But most times, our actions are responses to other root causes that involve families and friends. I am not telling you this in order to shift blame but suggesting that you widen your lens and understand that your actions may have made sense, considering the hurt, anger, fear, and anxiety that could have been operating within your relationship.

Can you give yourself a break for not having your act totally together? Can you learn from your mistakes and move on? Did your mother struggle with similar feelings and have the same coping skills? Sometimes we are surprised to learn that our mom can relate to us more than we think. She may have even walked in similar shoes.

Next, ask if this burden of guilt you carry is worth it. What benefit do you get from hanging on to these excessive feelings? Do you feel a need to punish yourself? Are you afraid to let go and act responsibly? Does guilt keep you distant from your mom?

Another step is to break the silence associated with your guilt and revisit your memory. Sometimes we have inaccurate perceptions or memories of what happened. For example, an adult daughter who spent years hanging on to guilt over her parents' divorce was sure she was the cause of their breakup. When she talked about the divorce with her mom in therapy, she learned that she'd had little to do with events that set the divorce in motion. Her mother was able to relieve her of this long-carried burden.

Related to this is assuming responsibility when it's not yours to assume. Guilt results when you see another person suffering or struggling and feel it is your responsibility to make the difficulties stop—but you can't. A good example of this is daughters who feel the tension of their parents' marital relationship and cope through food. Afraid their parents will divorce, and feeling out of control and helpless, they may develop an eating disorder. The eating disorder may bring the parents together to solve the daughter's eating problem. The daughter feels responsible to help her parents and thus remains sick. Marital tension is reduced because both parents are now working as a team to help their sick daughter.

Feeling responsible for others at the expense of yourself is a hallmark of an eating disorder. Usually it is motivated by feelings of helplessness.

As I continue to remind you throughout this book, you can only be responsible for you and your actions. When you get this, you will be able to release the guilt associated with feeling responsible for others.

Finally, releasing guilt is all about accepting the forgiveness that is offered to you by others and by God. Grace has nothing to do with what we deserve. It is a free gift offered by a loving God. All you have to do is accept it. And it's God's grace that allows us to walk and live in freedom. Accept forgiveness and walk in grace.

SHAME IS NOT ON YOU

Shame is different than guilt. Guilt is a response to something we believe we did wrong. It is a feeling of remorse for a real or imagined offense. "I did _____, and that was wrong." Shame, as mentioned before, is a feeling of being bad, a mistake, a loser.

Here are twenty questions that may help you identify the role of shame in your life. There is nothing scientific about these questions. They are just meant to help you think about shame and how it impacts your relationships.

1. Do I have a general feeling of being bad, unloved, or inadequate?

2. Do I find myself constantly belittling myself or being self-critical?

3. Do I avoid responsibility because I feel like I'll fail or be exposed?

4. Do I feel the urge to always rescue people or stand with the underdog?

5. Do I isolate myself because of the way I feel about myself?

6. Am I extremely sensitive and defensive?

7. Do I avoid looking at people when they talk to me?

8. Am I overly concerned with who is at fault?

9. Do I feel guilty a lot?

10. Do I harp on "my rights"?

11. Do I continue to bring up past mistakes?

12. On a regular basis, do I consider my own opinions and needs last?

13. Do I have a strong fear of failure?

14. Do I say I am wrong when I'm not?

15. Do I try to be perfect?

16. Am I compulsive in things I do?

17. Do I reject compliments?

18. Do I feel a need to give to others or they won't like me?

19. Do I get involved in unhealthy relationships and stay in them?

20. Do I stay silent about things I know to be wrong?

Shame is more serious than guilt. It is a thought, feeling, or belief related to being flawed. When we feel shame, we feel our very being is terrible, wrong, inadequate, and no good. Shame is often the fallout of abuse and rape. For example, a woman called in to a television talk show I was on and reported having intense feelings of shame. At the core of her feelings was a belief that if she had not been thin and attractive, she never would have been raped. Because she believed this, she gained an enormous amount of weight in order to keep potential predators away. Her flawed thoughts concerning responsibility for the rape led to shame.

Shame is an inner voice that keeps you silenced, fearful, anxious, and depressed. That voice is best silenced through an understanding of who you are in Christ. This includes your identity as well as the acceptance of forgiveness, grace, renewal, and the restoration promised by God. When we block out the voices of shame and listen only to the true voice of God, healing begins. In God's eyes we are worthy. When we feel shame, we need to check our thoughts—because God's thoughts are very different. For example:

1. *I am no good.* No, *your sin* is no good. When you repent, you live in God's grace. There is no goodness apart from God.

2. *I can't do it.* Maybe not, but *with* God all things are possible.

He will help you do what He has called you to do. There is no room for self-doubt, given His ability to equip you and empower you. You are not the lone ranger. In the words of James Taylor, "You've got a friend." And boy, does this friend empower and equip!

3. *I should* (fill in the blank), but I don't. "Shoulds" get us in trouble. Most of us *should* act certain ways, but we don't. We can feel ashamed, or we can accept God's grace and try again.

4. *I'm not loved because of my mistakes or inadequacies.* You are loved because God chose you. Acceptance is not based on what you do. His grace is sufficient.

5. *I am a mistake.* No, you were planned from the foundation of time. You are wonderfully made and created for a purpose. A created life is never a mistake.

Waiting in the Long Line for Approval

If you are still waiting to win your mother's approval, it's time to stop. You may never get it or be "good enough" in her eyes. One adult daughter I knew couldn't give up trying. For years, she did everything in her power to make her mother say, "You are a good daughter." But nothing she did ever won that confirmation. It never happened. And she lived much of her adult life depressed.

When she was finally ready to confront this loss, she realized how much time she had wasted trying to get approval from a woman who was incapable or unwilling to give it. Then the daughter realized that her need for acceptance could be met spiritually and by others. How exciting it was for her to learn the spiritual provision for love and acceptance through God.

God's love doesn't depend on our human nurturing or lack of nurturing experiences. God freely gives to all who come to Him. This woman only had to choose God. He had already chosen her.

THOUGHT POINTS

1. Identify those things you feel guilty about in your relationship with your mother.

2. Are there any issues over which you need to make peace with your mother? If so, do it!

3. Consider the differences between guilt and shame.

4. Do you hold judgment over your mother? If so, what can you do to release that judgment?

5. Do you feel responsible for your mother? If so, consider how you can renegotiate those responsibilities with her.

6. Have you violated your mother's trust? If so, what steps can you take to improve your relationship?

7. Do you constantly look for your mom's approval? Consider how you can relieve yourself of that pressure.

8. Are there shame issues in your family? An issue that has been kept silent? What could you do to break the silence and/or remove shame? (You may want to consider family therapy to help with this.)

II

THE GOOD-ENOUGH MOTHER:
THE IMPORTANCE OF HONOR

IT WAS A QUIET SUMMER DAY in June of 1972. I could finally relax after all the hoopla of graduation and my middle brother's recent wedding. In a few weeks, I would join my fellow students on a trip to Europe. Life was good and full of promise.

My older brother Gary, drafted into the army as an officer, had safely returned from Vietnam. Recently chosen to be part of an honorary mission around the world, he was flying home on the final leg of the seven-week tour. Meanwhile, his pregnant wife and two-year-old son were visiting our family.

It was a happy time in our family life. The oldest son had survived a war and now had a promising military career, the middle son was newly married and in the ministry, and I, the youngest and only daughter, was about to be launched into the college world.

After spending a lazy summer day with a friend, I headed back to my house. Excitement about my upcoming trip to Europe and college in the fall was building. I had been accepted at the University of Michigan and was following my older brother's footsteps. My family members were avid—no, make that *obsessed*, fans of the Maize and Blue. If you want to make the family proud, memorize the words to "Hail to the Victors" and become a Wolverine.

As I approached the driveway, I thought it rather odd that my father was home at midday. "Dad, what's up?" I asked as I walked through the door into the kitchen. His face was somber. And the fact that an unknown army officer was standing in the kitchen told me something was terribly wrong. Dad hesitated but then spoke, "Your brother is missing. His plane blew up over New Delhi, India, and there doesn't appear to be any survivors. We need to tell Mom and Wanda [his wife]."

Shocked and stunned, I couldn't speak. My brother was killed on an airplane after surviving a tour of duty in Vietnam? All the times he had been shot down and fired at during the war, and now his life ends with a *civilian* plane crash? I don't think so! This wasn't possible. He was no longer fighting a war, and his wife was about to have another baby. There must be some mistake. He was *missing* the officer had said, not *dead*.

"Linda, the plane blew up," Dad continued. "They haven't found any survivors. And the likelihood that they will . . . well, there is little room for hope at this point."

The days that followed were like a surreal nightmare. I kept thinking I would wake up from the bad dream and life would be back to normal. *I'll go to college, my family will enjoy the birth of the next grandson, and everything will be just fine.* But sitting at my brother's gravesite, listening to the haunting sound of taps, I knew life would never go back to "normal." It had been dramatically altered.

We never found out exactly what happened to my brother's commercial flight. It was believed to be the target of a terrorist bomb, blown up prior to landing, killing all the military brass on board. But the investigators never provided specifics. A bloody military dog tag, a wedding ring, a wallet, and parts of my brother's briefcase were proof that he had been on board and would never return to us.

Now, you may be wondering why I am telling you this traumatic story in a book about mothers and daughters? The reason has to do with how we heal and the role honor plays in our healing.

HONOR BRINGS HEALING

In the military, honor, sacrifice, and duty still matter. As grievous as my brother's death was, there was a deep sense of honor involved at his funeral—the men in uniform; the twenty-one-gun salute; the flag draped over the coffin; the slow, melancholy sound of the bugle playing taps; the marching; the saluting . . . it was all so moving and part of the healing.

Honor is valued in military life. It is given to those higher in the chain of command. And it's given to all who serve and die for our country. Honor is also highly valued by God. He speaks of it often from the Bible. "Honor your father and your mother" was one of the Ten Commandments given to the children of Israel; it was later repeated by Jesus in the New Testament. Here is what God says about honoring your mother (all scriptures are from the New American Standard Bible):

Exodus 20:12: "Honor your father and your mother, that your days may be prolonged in the land which the LORD your God gives you."

Exodus 21:17: "He who curses his father or his mother shall surely be put to death."

Leviticus 19:3: "Every one of you shall reverence his mother and his father, and you shall keep My sabbaths; I am the LORD your God."

Proverbs 1:8: "Hear, my son, your father's instruction and do not forsake your mother's teaching."

Proverbs 20:20: "He who curses his father or his mother, his lamp will go out in time of darkness."

Proverbs 23:22: "Listen to your father who begot you, and do not despise your mother when she is old."

Proverbs 30:17: "The eye that mocks a father and scorns a mother, the ravens of the valley will pick it out, and the young eagles will eat it."

Matthew 15:4: "For God said, 'Honor your father and mother,' and, 'He who speaks evil of father or mother is to be put to death.'"

Matthew 19:19: "Honor your father and mother; and you shall love your neighbor as yourself."

Mark 10:19: "You know the commandments, 'Do not murder, do not commit adultery, do not steal, do not bear false witness, do not defraud, honor your father and mother.'"

Scripture is clear that we owe honor to our mom. But do we do what Scripture commands? And anyway, why is it important to honor a mother?

During the writing of this book, the subject of honor kept coming to mind. My nephew Patrick was staying with us for a number of weeks while he finished his design concept for submission to the design competitions for the New York City World Trade Center Memorial Gardens. Patrick was the baby who was in utero when his father (my brother) died in the airplane explosion. As a designer, the chance to work on this project was the opportunity of a lifetime.

Because of Patrick's past (losing his father to a terrorist bomb), he was drawn to the project. His personal loss, along with his experience of being in New York City to meet with clients who had been at the World Trade Center when terrorists attacked on September 11, 2001, left an indelible impression on him. Intuitively, he resonated with the idea of creating a space for people to mourn their losses and to honor those who perished and were part of the rescue and recovery. It was part of his own healing journey. When 9/11 happened, he knew he had to be involved and spent many days just walking around ground zero.

As he developed his concept and began putting together his design for the memorial gardens, he drew heavily from his own experiences with loss. What would bring people together? How could we honor those who died in such horrific circumstances? The concept he settled on involved several paths for healing—remembrance, celebration, healing, hope—and honor. Honor brings healing.

I asked Patrick, "What happens in the space you've designed for honor?"

"There is a monument wall," he said. "It recognizes all the individual groups that participated during the rescue, recovery, and ongoing healing. There are sculptures of a 'Chain of Heroes' linking arms, representing unity during tragedy. And there is a 'Circle of Honor' that is a visual extension of the memorial gardens, allowing those who enter the site to continue through other paths of hope, healing, remembrance, and celebration. Honor is a path to healing—but also a thread throughout the entire memorial."

The people who died that day on 9/11 were ordinary people living their ordinary lives. One of the ways we heal from their losses is to find a way to honor these ordinary people. Their lives weren't perfect. They may not have been terribly important people in terms of celebrity, but their lives mattered and need to be remembered. And we, the people who knew them or knew of them, need to honor them.

As Patrick and I talked more about the importance of honor, it struck me that honor does bring healing. And I realized that honor is involved in every healthy relationship between mother and daughter. In order for daughters to heal and come to terms with their grown-up lives, they must come to terms with their losses and find ways to honor their mother.

All daughters experience loss in their mother-daughter relationship. Whether it's the loss of a dream, an expectation, a relationship, or a situation, loss is a part of growing up and becoming your own person. Why is loss a part of the relationship? Because there are no perfect mothers who did everything right. There are only "good-enough" mothers.

Author Judith Viorst wrote this about mothers: "We will have to give up the hope that, if we try hard, we somehow will always do right by our children. The connection is imperfect. We will sometimes do wrong."[1] It's true. Mothers sometimes do wrong. And when they do, daughters must grieve, forgive, and accept those losses in order to have a healthy relationship with Mom. And through this process, daughters must also find ways to honor their imperfect mother.

As Patrick worked week after week on the World Trade Center project, I began to think more about healing and honor as we discussed ways to remember, celebrate, and provide hope. In order to heal, to make peace, and to be at peace, we must not only find ways to honor those who have fallen, but those still with us.

Mothering involves sacrifice, nurturing, caring, teaching, empowering, and so much more. We usually expect mothers to do it all well and do it perfectly. When they don't, we are prone to anger, resentment, disappointment, and other negative emotions. But as we grieve the loss of the perfect mother, we heal. And as we heal, we find ways to bring honor to the woman who gave us life and was responsible for our very existence. Healing and honor are intertwined.

According to Webster, honor is "the testimony of esteem; any expression of respect or of high estimation by words or actions. It can also mean reverence, reputation, to revere, to respect, to treat with deference or submission."[2]

Honoring your mother may or may not be an easy thing to do. As you move through life, continually gaining more acceptance of the woman your mother is, tell her how much you appreciate her, say kind things to her, or talk to her about her good points. Let her know you love her and respect the difficulty of her job. Mothers need to hear these kinds of things!

Reflect on those moments in your relationship that were affirming, nurturing, and caring. Then design your own ways to honor her. If you need some help, here are a few suggestions to get you started:

1. Call her and tell her one thing you remember that she did right.

2. List several examples of loving or happy times you had with your mom, then, if possible, share the list with her.

3. Take a step to resolve your differences or past hurts.

4. Write a poem about your mother. Give it to her on a special day or just because you were thinking of her.

5. Write a short story about you and your mother and share it with her.

6. Make a short visit just to tell her you love and appreciate her.

7. Send a card for no reason, just to let her know you are thinking about her.

8. Put together a small scrapbook of pictures of you with your mom—fond memories you can visually review.

9. Watch an old family video of a happy time.

10. Pull out your baby pictures and talk to her about your birth.

11. Share happy memories of any family occasion.

12. Remember her on important dates like her birthday, Mother's Day, and Christmas.

13. Take her dinner or buy her flowers for no special reason.

14. Make an effort to talk about positive things she does that you appreciate versus focusing on her imperfections.

15. Tell her you love her and appreciate the sacrifices she has made over the years.

16. Take her shopping, to a movie, to a tearoom, or somewhere you can create a happy memory.

17. Invite her to a family picnic or get-together.

18. Tell her you understand how difficult it is to be a mom.

19. Forgive her.

20. Include her in something that shows her talent and gifts.

When Honor Is Hard to Find

The harder question, and the one more daughters struggle with, is how to honor a mom who has hurt or failed them in some way. It's those imperfect connections that make us struggle—the unfulfilled expectations, the unrealized dreams, the unmet needs. Most of us have these "issues" that keep tripping us up in our mother-daughter relationship.

Stacy was one of those daughters searching for answers. As the family planned how they would celebrate Mom's fiftieth birthday, Stacy, the middle child, was asked to "say something" special about her mom at the party. Her older sister was taking care of the party arrangements and preferred to contribute behind the scenes. Stacy, her two siblings insisted, was the eloquent and polished speaker of the family. Thus, they assumed she would be the family spokesperson for the birthday party. Stacy was definitely the one who should give the speech, everyone said.

"My dear siblings," Stacy responded, "aren't you forgetting one major important point here? Mom basically hates me and blames me for her now-miserable life!"

"We know, Stacy," her sister said. "But she's wrong, and you are great at giving speeches. Remember your high school graduation? You were the best! You can do this. Forget about 'the problem' and just do it."

"Easy for you guys to say!" Stacy answered. But she agreed to do it. Then, as she prepared for the party, she struggled with what to say. Her mom had wanted nothing to do with organized religion after her divorce from Dad. Stacy's father had claimed to be a Christian—and then ran off with his secretary, leaving the family in deep financial distress. The anger her mom felt at his hypocrisy turned her away from God. Religion, Stacy's mom now proclaimed, was for the weak and for those who needed an excuse to not take responsibility for themselves.

Embittered by the divorce, Stacy's mother blamed Stacy for part of the problem. You see, Stacy had known about her father's secret affair but had been sworn to silence. Her dad had promised to end the affair and confess to his wife. So Stacy waited silently, believing her father would come clean and do as he said he would. But he didn't. Instead, he ended up betraying both his daughter and his wife.

Devastated by the betrayal, Stacy sought her mom's comfort. But all she found was blame and anger. "How dare you not tell me what was going on and make me look like a fool!" her mother cried. "I'll never forgive you for this!" Those words left an imprint on Stacy's brain and rang in her head for months. In fact, it took a therapist to help relieve her of the misplaced guilt she carried.

Things went from bad to worse. Mom refused to speak to Stacy for months. She hung up the phone whenever she heard Stacy's voice. Despite all her efforts and an invitation to join Stacy in therapy, Stacy remained the target for Mom's anger and bitterness. It wasn't until Evan, Mom's boyfriend, came along that Mom even reacknowledged Stacy's existence. "Give me some time with her," Evan suggested to Stacy. "She's really angry at your dad, not at you. It wasn't your fault. You were just an easy target."

Evan somehow managed to break the ice with Mom. Although her mom hadn't apologized for how she treated Stacy, and although she continued to blame Stacy for the divorce, she was willing to allow her to come to the birthday party. At least that was a beginning step toward reconnection.

Perhaps if Stacy gave a rousing speech, her siblings thought, their mom would be willing to talk about what happened. Convinced it was a bad idea, Stacy tried to decline; but her siblings were insistent, begging, "Come on, Stacy, you can do this. You be the one to honor Mom on this important day. We want you to do it, and we are behind you. Mom can't stay mad at you forever."

"Oh, yeah? She still thinks I'm at fault," Stacy replied. "How do I honor her when she's so hateful to me? Do I pretend nothing ever happened and we are one happy family?"

"No. We aren't asking you to pretend anything. We just want you to be the grownup and do the right thing," her brother insisted. "Come on, sis, this is what our faith is all about. Treat her the way you would want to be treated. I know it won't be easy, but it's a step in the right direction."

"But I don't want to treat her nicely when she's been so awful to me! I have feelings too, you know. What about me and the way I've been wronged?" Stacy protested. "I've put up with her anger for months now. It's unfair. She doesn't understand the position Dad put me in and how he lied to me. And she won't let me talk to her about it. She's a grownup too. In fact, she was a grownup first!"

"I know," her sister tried to comfort her. "But remember what we were taught to believe. And despite Dad's mess, we still have to be responsible to God for our actions and thoughts. Remember what they did to Jesus, Stacy. They betrayed Him. He did nothing wrong and was treated horribly. But He still forgave and had compassion on us. He tells us to do the same. Honor her because it is the right thing to do, not because it *feels* right. Think about Jesus's words, 'Honor your father and your mother.' I'm not trying to put guilt on you, but I think we have to step up to the plate when she's not thinking right. We haven't thrown our faith out the window, and maybe she needs to see some Christians acting right. You will be the bigger person and grow from this. Focus on what Mom was like before the divorce, the times she helped us and was there for us. She was a good mom and not an angry person before the divorce. Try to remember her good points and then present that as a gift of love to her, expecting nothing in return. You will benefit from your obedience to God's Word."

Her sister was right, and Stacy knew it. She always hated that her sister was so reasonable. While Stacy was off having tantrums and being "emotional," her sister remained the steady one, always knowing how to calm her down. "OK, but this is going to be hard," Stacy said. "You guys start praying for me now and don't stop until I finish my last word at the party."

Later, Stacy sat down at the computer to compose her "speech" and stared at the screen. Then she prayed. "OK, here I go. What on earth do I say to a woman who has basically disowned me because of my dad, and has never apologized and simply tolerates my presence? God, do you really expect me to do this?"

She picked up the Bible off her desk. *Maybe I can find some condi-*

tion that exempts me from saying nice things about Mom because of the way I've been treated, she thought. Instead she opened the Bible to Ephesians 6:2–3 and read, "'Honor your father and mother' is the first commandment that has a promise attached to it, namely, 'so you will live well and have a long life'" (MSG). She knew there was no special condition.

The verse didn't say, "Honor your mother only if she's good to you," or "Honor her only if she has treated you fairly." As she read the study notes for this scripture, she realized that honor is an act of obedience and is the will of God. It was an inward reverence that God expected her to have, not based on her mother's behavior but based on love. "God so loved the world that he gave. . . ."[3] She, too, needed to give at this important occasion.

So she thought about her life and the role her mother had played in it thus far. Prior to the divorce, her mother was extremely devoted to the family. She laughed, played games, and took time to be with her children. Stacy had many fond memories of vacations, fun days, and her mother being by her side.

She thought about her mother's secret desire to be an artist and how she had talked about pursuing her art when the children were grown. As Stacy rummaged through some old pictures she had saved, she found one that had special meaning. It was a beautiful floral drawing her mother had given her. *This would make a perfect party invitation cover! she thought to herself. What a surprise it would be for her to see this on the invitation.*

Stacy began to write about her mother's influence in her own love for art. As Stacy thought about the things her mother did to impact her life positively, the list began to grow. And then she turned to another verse in her Bible, Philippians 4:8, and read, "Summing it all up, friends, I'd say you'll do best by filling your minds and meditating on things true, noble, reputable, authentic, compelling, gracious—

the best, not the worst; the beautiful, not the ugly; things to praise, not things to curse" (MSG).

Yes, her mother had unfairly displaced anger and blame onto Stacy for her divorce. And yes, Stacy had every right to be upset, and she wasn't in denial about the problem. But this day, she chose to think on good things about her mother despite the unfair treatment. Her memory could recall times of "good mothering." And that was what she would honor.

The day of the party arrived. Stacy was so nervous she could hardly read what she had written. As she anxiously approached the microphone and thanked all the guests for coming, she turned to her mom and began, "This is the woman who gave me life, an appreciation for art, and memories of laughter and fun." The anxiety dissipated. Stacy continued, "It is a day to honor her and to tell all of you how much she means to our family. My mother isn't perfect, and interestingly enough, neither are any of her children. We've all made mistakes, but at the core of our imperfections has always been a deep love.

"When my brother, sister, and I were young, my mother made many sacrifices. Most of you don't know that she gave up an art scholarship to parent the three of us. She has talent, and we wanted you to see it in its early form. The invitation you received for this party was one of my mother's early works. Isn't it beautiful? It was my mother's love for art that inspired me to be a designer. She opened up a world of beauty and color I had never known.

"Like so many mothers do, Mom put her desires and interests on hold to further ours. It was a sacrifice we so appreciated. Thank you, Mom, for always being available to us and for schlepping us around the park, to soccer practice, to art lessons, to play dates, to school activities. Not only did you taxi us, but you were always at the event, cheering us on and encouraging our dreams. All of us attribute our success to your constant encouragement. You never told us what we couldn't do. Instead, you encouraged us to dream about what we wanted to do and go after it.

"Mom, you taught me so much! The most important lesson I learned was how to be tough and endure difficulty, to never give up and keep trying, even when things didn't work out the way I hoped. Your example is the reason I stand here today. It's not in me to be defeated by life. The reason we keep going has everything to do with the legacy of faith you gave us. Faith in God is what pulled us through our many difficulties. And for that legacy of faith, I am eternally grateful.

"I've yet to become a mother. But I have a small sense of how difficult the job must be. I know that when a mother experiences her own emotional pain, she can never really do it alone. Her children are always with her, a part of her. And thus, a mother often gives up her individual rights for the rights of others. Somehow, her example helped us better understand Christ's directive to lay down our life for another.

"Well, I could go on, but we have a party to attend to here. Thank you, Mom, for teaching us so much, for being available to us, and for helping us dream. You are a big part of who I am today. And with all my flaws, I'd say you did a pretty good job. OK, you can applaud here.

"On this important day of honoring your birth, your children would like to honor you for giving birth. Three lives would like to applaud your efforts and tell you that we love you. The investment you made in your children has brought forth fruit. Happy fiftieth birthday, Mom. May the peace of God rule in your heart, and may He fill you with His everlasting love."

Stacy stood very still. For a moment, she was her mother's daughter, bringing honor to the position and to the memories of times past. As she folded her paper and moved slowly back to her chair, she glanced at her mother's face and noticed a tear running down her cheek. Then Stacy began to cry. Her mother wasn't perfect; in fact, her mother's action toward her had been wrong. But because Stacy was willing to honor her mother despite the ongoing problems, healing began. Her mother was moved by her daughter's godly obedience. It was time to reconnect with her daughter again. In fact, it was time to apologize and make amends.

Stacy's motivation to honor her mom was not based on the promise of a long life, although that is the promise mentioned in Scripture. Stacy understood a deeper truth, one many daughters fail to grasp. She realized how much God loved her when she behaved in wrong ways or made mistakes. God wasn't interested in her perfection as a condition to lavish His love on her. He honors her just because she is His daughter.

There are times when daughters may be the ones called upon to be patient and loving. Yes, we may be treated unfairly. During those times, the challenge is to still honor our mom. This doesn't mean we become doormats for emotional abuse and never assert ourselves or set limits. It only means that we must be careful in our responses and not be quick to act out of anger. Sometimes we need to be more empathetic and cut our mom some slack.

A woman I knew really brought this point home to me. She had a tragic past characterized by abuse and deep hurts. But in those times when her mother was stable and not acting mentally ill, they had moments of loving mother-daughter interactions. Those were the moments the daughter chose to focus upon. Her understanding of mental illness didn't make it any easier to be the target of her mother's instability. But she realized that her mother's times of fleeting lucidity represented the woman God intended the mother to be. As the daughter grieved the many losses involved with having a mentally ill mother, she cherished the positive times and gave honor to her mom where she could.

To honor someone means to give the person high respect. We can all honor our mother for giving us life and doing the best she knew how to do. No matter what the status of your relationship with your mother, she is the one who brought you into this world. The decision to honor her is not based on her performance or your personal score card. It is an act of obedience to God.

If you don't have much of an intimate mother-daughter relationship and there are serious issues between the two of you, you might consider therapy to help move you through grief and into acceptance. So often, daughters stay in that hurt little girl position and never assume their grownup identities. If your mom refuses to be a part of the healing, work on your reactions. Your healing doesn't depend on how she acts or doesn't act.

Once you understand the family patterns that have led to dysfunction, the idea is to break them and not become an unconscious repeater. The work you must do is similar to peeling the layers of an onion. First you deal with a few things, peeling away the outer layers of relationship issues. Then you do more. As you remove the various layers, you get closer to the core. The more layers you peel, the more intense your reactions. A core issue for mother-daughter relationships is to find ways to be interdependent while recognizing our individual fallibilities. We can't be forever dependent on our mom or expect her to anticipate our needs or continue to take care of us. But we can honor her for her efforts.

If your mother doesn't change, refuses to ask for forgiveness, doesn't appear mentally stable, doesn't handle stress well, or chooses not to control her unbridled emotions, grieve those losses. But in the process of grieving, find a way to honor her.

All mothers make sacrifices, and daughters need to say thank you. Honor is not about having a great childhood or about having a mom who got it all right. Honor is about gratitude and respect for the difficulty of the job.

Still Too Dependent?

In the Bible, the children of Israel had a long history of dependence based on disappointment. They had a great leader, Moses, but leaned on him too much. When something went wrong, they complained and wanted Moses to rectify the situation. They expected him to speak to God and take care of the problem. Regularly they reminded Moses of their suffering in the wilderness and blamed him for taking them out of Egypt. Despite the repeated miracles of God, they chose to stay dependent on Moses, not on God. Does this remind you at all about the way we think of our mother?

Joshua 1 begins with the Lord saying to Joshua, "Moses is dead. Arise!"[4] God told Joshua, "It's your turn, and here are My promises." Moses was gone. Joshua could no longer depend on him, even if he wanted to. Joshua depended on God and believed His promises.

If your mom is a Moses in your life, God's Word to you is, "Moses is dead." It's time for you to arise and stop depending on her and blaming her for all your problems.

Quit complaining about what didn't happen in your life. Don't dwell on all the ways you have been wronged. Think about Joshua. He was an ex-slave who was led around the desert for years. Despite his problems, he trusted God, not the great leader of his people. We need to do the same. Your Mother Moses will let you down at some point in your life. It may be deliberate or it may be accidental, but disappointment will happen. It's time to stop looking to her to fix your life or make you feel better. Honor what she gave you, but move on with your life.

Forget Moses. I've Got Goliath to Fight!

Mary looked at me and said, "There is no way I can honor my mother. You know my history. That woman is a crazy person. She dominates my life. She's bigger, stronger, and more powerful than I am. I can't even begin to think about honoring her. I just want to survive her. You are asking too much."

I told her, "Mary, remember the story of David and Goliath? Mightier army, better battle gear, bigger guy who mocked and taunted the Israelites? It's not just a story for kids. Goliath was a formidable enemy. David should have been mincemeat. But he wasn't. Why did David beat the giant? Because God was on his side."

Then I gave her another example, the story told in 2 Kings 6, when the great Syrian army surrounded the Israelites in the city of Dothan. When Elisha's servant saw all the horses and chariots waiting to strike at them, he asked Elisha what they should do. Elisha responded, "Do not fear, for those who are with us are more than those who are with them."[5] That reassurance seemed a bit bizarre, considering that Elisha could see the enemy and knew his people were in deep trouble.

But Elisha knew God was on his side, and he saw the battle with spiritual eyes. He prayed for his young servant to see the horses and chariots of fire all around them on the mountain. The eyes of the young servant were opened, and he saw God defending them.

When you face a difficult situation like my client Mary did, open your spiritual eyes and know that God is with you. His promise is to be on your side, no matter who or what comes against you. God will help you respond to your mom with respect and bless your decision to honor her.

Mary's challenge was to react in a godly way to her mom. In the natural way of things, she wanted to get revenge and expose her lies. And she had every right to want that. But she chose God's way instead of her own. Instead of anger and revenge, she chose peace, righteousness, faith, and honor. She knew God would help her, even though the odds were against her. She prayed often and intensely. She needed power to be lovely to her difficult mom.

You can operate in the same confidence as Mary. God is on your side and will help fight your battles for you. Go to Him when you feel overwhelmed and need victory. Stand firm on His Word, and believe He is there, ready to fight for you. Then rest in His promise that He will honor your obedience.

What Difference Does It Make?

Perhaps you've said, "What difference does it make whether or not I honor my mother? I'm going to take talk radio's advice and cut her off if she treats me poorly. I don't have to put up with her nonsense. She'll get what she deserves. This honor talk is ridiculous and out-dated."

All I can say is, I didn't write the Ten Commandments. The walk of faith is motivated by our desire to please God, not by our individual feelings or even beliefs. It's easy to cut off a difficult relationship. It's much harder to stay in it and be loving.

And here's a news flash: Very few people will congratulate you when you decide to act godly. They may even tell you that you are a fool. But Jesus's words are radical and often counter the cultural attitude.

There is a reward for your obedience to God. Psalm 19:8–11 says,

> The precepts of the LORD are right,
>   giving joy to the heart.
> The commands of the LORD are radiant,
>   giving light to the eyes.
> The fear of the LORD is pure,
>   enduring forever.
> The ordinances of the LORD are sure
>   and altogether righteous.
> They are more precious than gold,

> than much pure gold;
>> they are sweeter than honey,
>>> than honey from the comb.
>> By them is your servant warned;
>>> in keeping them there is great reward.

The psalmist reminds us to fear (meaning, to be reverent and obedient to) the Lord and live a life pleasing to God. When we keep God's commandments, we will be rewarded. He also says our reward will be great.

Obedience isn't easy. That's why Paul wrote in Galatians 6:9 that we are not to grow weary while doing good. He said that, in due season, if we don't lose heart, we will reap the reward of our actions. His words were meant to encourage us, to help us hang in there when it looks like nothing is happening.

I often have to remind myself that God talks about seasons—times to plant and times to reap. The benefit of honoring our mother is not always immediate. Yet the promises to live well and have a long life are given.

God Doesn't Play Hide-and-Seek

When my children were little, we played hide-and-seek. It's a game all children love. One night, young Katie took her turn to hide. We searched and searched but couldn't find her. She picked a really good hiding spot. At first, we were challenged by her ingenuity. Later, we all got frustrated and eventually gave up looking for her. "Game over!" we yelled. "Time to show yourself." She silently squealed with delight. No one could find her.

When mother-daughter relationship problems don't resolve quickly or to our liking, we often feel God isn't helping and can't be found. He's hiding. We say to ourselves, *I've prayed. That didn't do any good. Things are still the same. I don't really feel like God is helping me or that He's even here.* We give up and get depressed.

The truth is, God *doesn't* hide. He takes great pleasure in helping us.

In the Old Testament, David faced a situation in which He decided to seek God. First Samuel 30 describes how the Amalekites attacked the city of Ziklag. They burned the city then carried away all the residents, including the wives and families of David and his men. When David arrived and saw the destruction, he and his men wept. The city was destroyed, their families, including David's two wives, had been taken, and now his men were talking about stoning him. Talk about a bad day!

But the way David responded to his grim circumstances was important. He asked God what he should do next. Destruction, devastation, and loss all around him, David didn't know what to do. But instead of giving up or crying, "Woe is me," he turned to God and said, "Help!" And David believed God would answer.

And God did. He said, "Pursue, for you shall surely overtake them and without fail recover all."[6] In his distress, David sought God and asked what to do. He knew God would answer.

If we seek God, He shows us what to do. God doesn't go into hiding when we need answers.

If you are struggling to find ways to honor your mom because the relationship is difficult, ask God for help. Don't give up if the answer isn't immediately evident. Sometimes we have to wait and not grow weary. Pray, wait, and persist.

Resist the Urge to Give Up

Maybe you feel like giving up. This relationship stuff is just too intense, and you don't need the headache. Maybe you're saying, "I'm just going to forget about it. I can live my life avoiding my mom or seeing her on my terms. This relationship is too exhausting. I don't have the time or energy for it."

Well, don't give in to despair, no matter how bleak things look. You are on a journey that God wants to help you complete. It's easy to become discouraged as we go through life. Our natural tendency is to complain and grumble when things don't go our way. Our society encourages such behavior. But we need to look at biblical examples so we can understand how to handle disappointment and delay.

The best example I can think of involves the children of Israel, God's chosen people. God miraculously intervened in their lives— freed them from slavery, parted the Red Sea so they could pass, provided manna and quail daily to feed them. You know the story. Yet their response to the first sign of difficulty was to grumble and complain. Be honest; many of us are like that. When something goes wrong, we are quick to doubt God and let go of His Word, saying, "See, my mom will never change. What's the use? What's the point of trying?"

The lesson to learn from the children of Israel is that their grumbling and complaining led them to wander in the wilderness and prevented them from entering the Promised Land. If you feel you are wandering in a relationship desert, learn from the Israelites.

Philippians 2:13–14 tells us that God works in us for His good pleasure and that we are to do all things without complaining and disputing. He wants us to have all His promises, including healthy relationships, but we can block the process by grumbling and complaining, which are signs of doubt and unbelief. Rarely do we accomplish anything without a few obstacles along the way. When you run into difficulty in your relationship with your mother, do what God says, no matter how bad things look.

Honor and healing are intertwined. As we obey the commandment to honor our mother we need to remind ourselves that the commandment wasn't conditional. It's not, "Sarah, you give honor to your mom, but Jill, your mom messed up, so you're exempt." God's way doesn't work like that. God asks us all to honor our mother. Imperfect and fallible as she is, Mom is human—and gave birth to a fallible daughter. Whatever your struggles or your Mom issues, remember that "'Honor your father and mother' is the first commandment that has a promise attached to it, namely, 'so you will live well and have a long life.'"[7]

THOUGHT POINTS

1. Consider the commandment, "Honor your father and your mother." What do you think that scripture means?

2. Think of some specific examples of honor and how people are honored in our culture today.

3. Recall a positive memory that honors your mother. If you're in communication with your mother, tell her why it made such an impact. So often mothers only hear about what they did wrong, not right.

4. If you're aware of your mother's relationship with her mother, consider if and how she might have honored her mother. If possible, ask your mother to describe if and how she might have done things differently.

5. How does honoring our mother affect our relationship with God? Why do you think God made it a commandment?

Epilogue: You Can and Should Go Home Again

Probably the most surprising thing I learned while training to become a therapist was that relationship problems weren't all about one person. That may seem like an obvious revelation, but in reality, it isn't. When it comes to mother-daughter relationship problems, mothers still blame their insensitive daughters, daughters blame their overbearing mother, and the "it's her fault" tape continues to play loud and clear in therapy rooms all across the country. I hope after reading this book you have learned that the blaming game takes you nowhere and doesn't lead to the intimate connections we all desire.

Let's face it. Whenever we experience relationship difficulties, we want to believe the problem has nothing to do with us. And sometimes we vow to endure hell and high water to prove our point.

Thank goodness I've surrendered my stupidity! Would you like to join me?

I understand the complexities that mother-daughter relationships present. I know your mom has disappointed you, talks too much, gets in your business, and makes your life crazy. But she's your mother. Can you find a way to love her, to honor her, to pray for her, and to connect with her? It is my hope that you will try.

When you've read the last pages of this book, don't go back to life as it was before. Instead, ask God what you can do to deepen your mother-daughter connection. If you've been estranged, if you've given up or surrendered to the exhaustion of relationship work, try one more time using everything you've read here as a guide. It won't be easy, and it may take a great deal of patience on your part, but the bond that can result, even the moments of intimacy you may find, are worth the effort.

The journey home may take several trips, and those trips usually create intense emotions. Don't be afraid of them. Embrace and work through those emotions. Grieve what isn't; accept what is. Spend time together. Be willing to open up. Use your skills of empathy. Search for new connections. Create something new.

Also, keep this in mind as you consider the work you need to do: Our willingness to work through our imperfect mother-daughter connection is often influenced by our developmental stage in life. Author Judith Viorst provides a helpful development perspective when it comes to dealing with our mother. She says that in our twenties we establish our independence and tend to believe that we are not like our parents. In our thirties, we discover the resemblances that exist despite our resistance; we understand that Mom is somehow in us. And when we acknowledge our similarities, we can work on not repeating them. In our middle years, we daughters are more willing to try and bridge the gap. Grieving our losses and learning to accept what may never be takes work.[1] Take the time; make the effort. You won't regret it.

CREATED TO BE IN RELATIONSHIP

The life of faith is not an individual journey walked out on a lonely path. We were created to be in relationship with each other and with God. Our relationships are where we develop patience, longsuffering, kindness, gentleness, humility, love, and so many more Christlike characteristics.

Jesus repeatedly calls us to live in unity and be reconciled with one another. It is the heart of God that we love one another. And that love is to be given whether or not we are loved in return. Because Christ loves us, we are to love our mother with that same love.

Sole Survivor

Early in life, one young daughter discovered that love was all that mattered. It was a typical day at the airport in August 1987. Six crew members and 148 passengers boarded Northwest Airlines flight 255 scheduled to leave Detroit Metropolitan Airport bound for Phoenix, Arizona. But as the engines revved up and the plane began to lift off, something went terribly wrong. The McDonnell-Douglas MD-82 climbed approximately fifty feet, then stalled and crashed into several light posts and a rental car building. The remains of the plane skidded to a halt on an airport access road. Wreckage spewed from the site, killing two motorists who were driving along a nearby highway. The aircraft was reduced to a heap of metal and fire. Looking at the wreckage, there was little hope for any survivors.

As the Romulus, Michigan, firefighters picked their way through the debris, putting out fires and searching for clues, an amazing thing occurred. A firefighter heard a soft moan. Perhaps someone on the ground had been hit by the plane and was hurt. But as he made his way through the remains, he quickly realized the sound originated from within the wreckage of the airplane. There, strapped into a seat under the body of her dead mother, was a four-year-old girl who had miraculously survived the crash.

Sensing that something was terribly wrong with the airplane, the mother of little Cecilia had wrapped her body around her child and cushioned her from the tremendous forces of the crash. Nothing, not even death, would separate this mother from loving and protecting her daughter. Little Cecilia was the sole survivor of the crash.

The visual image of this mother's sacrifice is intense. It is a vivid picture of the depth of a mother's love for her daughter. And yet, this expression of motherly love is only a taste of the love God has for each of us.

If you feel as if you are a sole survivor of damaged relationships and family debris, please understand that God has His protective arms around you and won't relax His grip. He loves you. Nothing can separate you from His love. When you allow yourself to experience that love, your life will be changed.

THE SUPERNATURAL YEARNING

As daughters, we have to give up our dreams for the perfect mother-daughter connection and gratification. We must also recognize that the yearning that so beseeches us isn't entirely earthly. There is a deeper craving, a call from the Creator to be with Him. Unless we satisfy that yearning, we will always look to those we love to fill the void. And they can never really do that.

Human relationships remain imperfect with the hope and promise of eternal perfection. The oneness we experienced prior to birth is but a reminder of what will come someday. Meanwhile, we grow impatient if we don't satisfy this yearning through God. So look to God for the completeness you need and desire. In Him is perfect love that will calm your fear, restore your losses, and renew your spirit, because in Him we move and breathe and have our being. The yearning for perfect love is only met through intimacy with God. In that intimacy, we find the courage and the strength to work on our imperfect earthly connections.

As you contemplate the work that may still need to be done or as you celebrate the intimacies of your mother-daughter relationship, be encouraged. A mother's love can be the closest expression of God's love we may ever experience this side of heaven. As the apostle Paul described it,

> *Love suffers long and is kind; love does not envy; love does not parade itself, is not puffed up; does not behave rudely, does not seek its own, is not provoked, thinks no evil, does not rejoice in iniquity, but rejoices in the truth; bears all things, believes all things, hopes all things, endure all things. Love never fails.* (1 Corinthians 13:4–8, NKJV)

Love opens up possibilities. Because of love, you can and should go home again.

NOTES

Introduction: The Relationship That Affects All Others

1. Ephesians 6:2–3.
2. Betty Carter, "Legacies: Intergenerational Themes" a monograph published in cooperation with *Mothers and Daughters: The Women's Project in Family Therapy* (1981–82): 17.

1. *Now, Let's All Just Try to Stay Calm . . .*

1. See Galatians 5:16–26.

2. *Anger at Our Impossible Mothers*

1. The following biblical guideline points were adapted and revised from Linda Mintle, *Breaking Free from Anger and Unforgiveness* (Lake Mary, Fla.: CharismaHouse, 2002), 26–30.
2. Brad Bushman, Roy Baumeister, and Angela Stack, "Catharsis, Aggression and Persuasive Influence: Self-fulling or Self-defeating Prophecies?" *Journal of Personality and Social Psychology* 76, no. 3 (January 1999): 367–76.

Notes

3. Michael Elkin, *Families Under the Influence* (New York, London: Norton, 1990), 217.
4. Psalm 4:4.

4. Handling Conflict

1. Fingerman, *Mothers and Their Adult Daughters,* 105.
2. Ibid.
3. Ibid.

5. Great Expectations: Living Our Mother's Dream

1. Karen Fingerman, *Mothers and Their Adult Daughters: Mixed Emotions, Enduring Bonds* (Amherst, N.Y.: Promeseus, 2003), 50.
2. Elizabeth Debold, Marie Wilson, Idelisse Malave, *Mother-Daughter Revolution: From Betrayal to Power* (New York: Perseus, 1993), 41.
3. Margaret Wise Brown, *The Runaway Bunny* (New York: Harper & Row, 1942).

6. Growing Daughters: Making Meaningful Connections

1. J. L. Framo, "Family of Origin as a Therapeutic Resource for Adults in Marital and Family Therapy: You Can and Should Go Home Again," *Family Process* 15, No. 2 (1976): 193–210.

7. Families: The Ties That Define

1. Richard Simon, "The Family Unplugged: An Interview with Mary Pipher," *Family Therapy Networker*, January/February 1997, 24–34.
2. Ivan Bosozormenyi-Nagy and D. Ulrich cited in Linda Berg-Cross, *Basic Concepts in Family Therapy* (New York: Hawthorn Press, 1988), 165.

3. Carter, "Legacies: Intergenerational Themes," 16.
4. See Psalm 34:8.

8. *I Am My Mother—NOT!*

1. See Matthew 11:30.
2. See Matthew 10:39.
3. Peggy Papp, "Resolutions: Together Differently," a monograph published in connection with *The Women's Project on Family Therapy* (1981–82), 33.

9. *Forgiveness: The Healing Balm*

1. Susan Battley, quoted in B. Secunda, *Losing Your Parents, Finding Your Self* (New York: Hyperion, 2000), 236–37.
2. Robert D. Enright, *Human Development Study Group,* University of Wisconsin-Madison, 1991, http://www.newliferesourcesinc.com/forgiveness1.htm (accessed May 23, 2003).
3. See Luke 22:42.
4. Luke 23:34, KJV.
5. Max Lucado, *In the Grip of Grace* (Nashville: W Publishing, 1996), 36.

10. *The Good-Enough Daughter: Letting Go of Guilt and Shame*

1. Adapted from Luke 15, MSG.
2. Adapted from John 8:1–11.

11. *The Good-Enough Mother: The Importance of Honor*

1. Judith Viorst, *Necessary Losses: The Loves, Illusions, Dependencies and Impossible Expectations That All of Us Have to Give Up to Grow* (New York: Fawcett Gold Medal, Ballentine Books, 1987).

Notes

2. *Noah Webster's First Edition of an American Dictionary of the English Language*, republished in facsimile edition (San Francisco: Foundation for American Christian Education, 1995), 101–102.

3. John 3:16.

4. My paraphrase of the beginning of Joshua 1.

5. 2 Kings 6:16, NKJV.

6. 1 Samuel 6:8, NKJV.

7. Ephesians 6:2–3, MSG.

Epilogue: You Can and Should Go Home Again

1. Viorst, *Necessary Losses*, 255–56.